his Book Presented

DISCARD

The End of the Ancient World

An Illustrated History of the Church

Created and Produced by Jaca Book

The First Christians
From the beginnings to A.D. 180

The Church Established
A.D. 180—381

The End of the Ancient World
A.D. 381—630

The Formation of Christian Europe
A.D. 600—900

The Middle Ages
A.D. 900—1300

**The Breakdown
of Medieval Christendom**
A.D. 1300—1500

Protestant and Catholic Reform
A.D. 1500—1700

The Church in Revolutionary Times
A.D. 1700—1850

The Church and the Modern Nations
A.D. 1850—1945

The Church Today
A.D. 1945 and after

An outline by chapter can be found on the last two pages of this volume.

The End of the Ancient World

An Illustrated History of the Church

From 381 to 630

Translated and adapted by John Drury
Illustrated by Franco Vignazia

Winston Press   430 Oak Grove   Minneapolis, Minnesota 55403

Published in Italy under the title
L'ultimo mondo antico
Copyright © 1980 Jaca Book Edizioni

**Licensed publisher and distributor
of the English-language edition:**
Winston Press, Inc.
430 Oak Grove
Minneapolis, Minnesota 55403
United States of America

Agents:
Canada—
  LeDroit/Novalis-Select
  135 Nelson St.
  Ottawa, Ontario
  Canada KIN 7R4

Australia, New Zealand, New Guinea, Fiji Islands—
  Dove Communications, Pty. Ltd.
  203 Darling Road
  East Malvern, Victoria   3145
  Australia

United Kingdom, Ireland, and South Africa—
  Fowler-Wright Books, Ltd.
  Burgess St.
  Leominster, Herefordshire
  England

Created and produced by Jaca Book, Milan
Color selection: Carlo Scotti, Milan
Printing in TK Gorenjski tisk, Kranj

History Consultant: The Rev. Marvin R. O'Connell
                    Professor of History, University of Notre Dame

Winston Staff: Florence Flugaur, Meredith Montgomery—editorial
               Chris Larson, Keith McCormick—design

Library of Congress Catalog Card Number: 79-67832
ISBN: 0-03-056826-9

5 4 3 2 1

An Illustrated History of the Church

The End of the Ancient World
Introduction

The End of the Ancient World gives an account of how the Christian people passed through the tumultuous years when the Greek and Latin civilization collapsed after eight centuries and gave way to something new. The Eastern Empire survived, but it had ever less to do with its Roman origins. In the West, wave after wave of barbarian invaders broke through the imperial frontiers, until a hodge-podge of Germanic kingdoms replaced Rome's political and economic unity.

The process of disintegration was a long one, and gradually the old system's literary, engineering and organizational skills were lost. For the Christian people of western Europe, the fall of the empire presented special problems. Some of the conquering tribes were pagan and some were Arian. This meant that the important task of bringing people to the faith and love of Christ became even more difficult than before.

It stands as a monument to the courage and steadfastness of the Christian people of those times that their faith did not falter in this time of trouble. They were determined to keep all of the truth of their faith. In the West, they patiently strove to convert their German conquerors, while in the East, in a series of great councils, they preserved intact the revelation of Jesus' dual nature, human and divine, and his unique personality.

Christians of this era were blessed with some of the greatest leaders in all of Christian history: John Chrysostom, Augustine of Hippo, Jerome, Benedict, and Scholastica. But this story goes far beyond these magnificent personalities and testifies to the Church's serene confidence that its mission goes on just the same, whatever severe changes come to society. For the Christian religion is for all times and all places and all people.

Marvin R. O'Connell

1. The Roman Empire faced troubled times around the year 400.

The Roman Empire was now ruled by Christian emperors. Its capital had been moved from Rome in the West to Constantinople in the East. This city had been built by Constantine the Great on the site of an ancient city called Byzantium. From this name the Eastern Roman Empire took its name: the Byzantine Empire. From Constantinople the emperors, with the help of their assistants, ruled territories in Europe, the Middle East, and northern Africa. The empire extended to parts of the huge land area known as Africa-Eurasia— mainly to areas bordering the Mediterranean Sea.

Constantinople had been built as a new city. It was clearly a Christian city, as it had no pagan temples such as those that could be seen in Rome. Located on a narrow strip of land between the Mediterranean Sea and the Black Sea, Constantinople was a rich and prosperous city. Its fine harbor helped make the city a successful center of business. Products from many places reached Constantinople by sea and by land, and its good location and strong defenses protected it from invaders. Under the emperor's protection, orthodox or Catholic Christianity became the religion of more and more people.

The living situation was far different in the western regions of the empire. Some areas were very poor and could not provide enough food for the people.

During the fourth century, certain Germanic tribes— allies of Rome— had been

allowed into the western part of the empire. These tribes spoke their own languages, and to Greeks and Romans these languages sounded strange and even crude—something like "bar-bar-bar." From this came the name *barbarian,* by which the tribes were called. The word *barbarian* came to mean people who were crude, uneducated, and on a lower scale of civilization than the people of the empire.

The barbarian allies had been granted land of their own within the Western Empire. Soon these tribes wanted more land. They gradually began moving out into imperial territory, took control over local people, and demanded acceptance from the emperors. In the far West, the people of Britain, Gaul, and Spain felt far removed from imperial rule and protection. City life in the West was falling apart and disappearing.

2. John Chrysostom was the finest Christian preacher of his day. As bishop of Constantinople, he was popular because of his simple, holy life. But he spoke out against the empress, and she had him exiled.

John Chrysostom— that is, John "of the golden mouth"—lived during the late fourth century. He was the finest preacher of his day, and it seems that only Origen in the third century wrote more works than John did. In his many sermons and writings, John tried to explain the books of the Bible. A liturgy— the prayers for the canon of the Mass— bears his name, but may not have been written by him.

John was born into a wealthy and respectable family of Antioch around 344. After his father died, John's mother guided his education until he went to study under Libanius, a famous teacher of rhetoric. (Rhetoric is the art of speaking and writing well.) A spirited youth and a fine talker, the young John enjoyed life in the upper circles of Antioch.

After thinking seriously about his life and talking to the great teacher Basil, John decided to lead a life of solitude and sacrifice for God. In 375 he withdrew to the hills near Antioch. For four years he studied the Bible under the direction of an old monk. Then he lived alone in a cave for two more years. He finally returned to Antioch to be ordained a deacon in 381 and a priest in 386. His fame as a preacher spread far and wide. Thus it was that in 397 Arcadius, the eastern emperor, named John bishop of Constantinople. During the six years he served as bishop, John won the favor of many people through his preaching and his apostolic work.

But John Chrysostom had enemies. Bishop Theophilus of Alexandria had wanted to be bishop of Constantinople, and he now worked against John. The empress, Eudoxia, disliked John because of his stand for morality, which she felt was critical of her.

In 403, a synod of thirty-five bishops met in Constantinople. Most of the bishops had been chosen by Theophilus because they were against John. They accused John of heresy and other crimes. He was found guilty and sent into exile. The people reacted angrily to this step, and John was recalled very quickly. But the very next year he was forced into exile again because his plain speaking made the empress angry. Due to the hardships he endured, he died in exile three years later. The people protested against John's successors until 438—thirty years later—when his remains were brought back and solemnly buried in Constantinople.

3. To explain what life was like around the year 400, we will imagine a story about a teenager named Andreas who lived in Constantinople. Andreas was a student, and after classes he liked to watch the chariot races.

To give a picture of what life was like for ordinary people at this time, we will tell the story of Andreas, an imaginary teenager who lived in Constantinople.

Andreas was seventeen, and he went to school, where he studied geometry, arithmetic, and oratory. He did not like the first two subjects, though he knew that he would need arithmetic when he began to work full time for his father, who was a merchant. Already Andreas helped at the family shop during busy times, unloading orders of cloth, spices, and earthenware.

Andreas liked to study oratory. In this subject he learned to express himself well and to speak convincingly, so that he could persuade others to believe and act as he wanted them to. Andreas also studied music and natural science, and the ancient classical writers, such as Vergil.

Of course, school did not take up all the time for Andreas and his friend. They often went to the hippodrome to enjoy themselves. The hippodrome was a huge, circular arena where chariot races were held. It was in the center of the city, right behind the imperial palace.

To get there from school, Andreas and his friends passed an arcade of bankers, where traders from many countries exchanged their money for the imperial coins of the Eastern Empire. Near this street was an intersection known as the "Vale of Tears" where slaves were sold. Often, these slaves had been captured in wars or kidnapped from other countries.

At the hippodrome, the charioteers lined up close to the barricade. People crowded close around them, placing bets on their favorites. But Andreas and his friends had no money for bets. They just enjoyed the excitement and shouted encouragement to their favorite team as the race began.

4. Andreas, the teenager
in our imaginary story,
was given his first
big job. He was to take
a cargo of precious cloth
from Constantinople
to Aquileia
in the Western Empire.
Andreas felt happy
and excited, but he felt
a little frightened, too.

When Andreas came home on the day of the chariot race, his mother told him to hurry to his father's place of business near the harbor. Andreas set off right away. As he neared his father's shop, he saw several camels loaded with goods standing outside.

The merchants who had brought the camel caravan were inside talking with Andreas's father. They had brought a load of precious Chinese cloth over the "Silk Road," which was the name merchants gave the road from China to Constantinople. The Silk Road went over mountains, through cities, and across plains. Often caravan drivers had to fight off robbers and endure extreme heat and cold.

Andreas's father had an order for this particular load of cloth from a merchant in the Western Roman Empire, in the city of Aquileia. And Andreas was to be in charge of taking the cloth there.

Andreas had always known that someday he would begin to work as a merchant, like his father. But he couldn't help feeling

frightened as he thought of this, his first big job. First, there was the sea voyage from Constantinople across the Mediterranean to Aquileia, a large seaport in what is today northern Italy. Andreas would be responsible for the safety of the precious cargo on the voyage. Then, in Aquileia, he would have to deliver the cargo to the merchant Paul, who had ordered it, and collect the payment. The ship would be managed by an experienced sea captain and good crew of sailors, but Andreas felt that much depended on him. As he sat at the table with the merchants, he felt eager and brave, and also worried and afraid.

When the day came for him to leave, Andreas's mother gave him a small book of the Gospels. She told him to remember that no matter how far away he was, she would be praying for him. Andreas shook hands with his father and hugged him, too. Then the boat moved away from shore, and Andreas looked across the blue waters. He was on his way to Aquileia, his destination in the West.

5. Andreas, the young merchant
in our imaginary story,
arrived in Aquileia
with his cargo of cloth.
He looked forward
to seeing this city,
because it was
his first visit
to the Western Empire.
He was surprised
to find that Aquileia
was poor and run down.

The voyage from Constantinople to Aquileia went quickly, but Andreas had time to think about what he expected to see there. This was his first trip to the Western Empire, and he was excited to think that he would be in the land of some of the ancient Roman writers he had studied in school, such as Vergil, Cicero, and Horace. He expected Aquileia to be a rich bustling town. He knew that an army fortress was there, built one hundred years ago by Emperor Diocletian. And in shops in Constantinople, he had often seen expensive amber pieces and purple cloth that had come from Aquileia.

The boat docked, and Andreas went ashore with the sea captain, who would help him find Paul, the merchant. As they walked through the streets, Andreas was surprised to see that Aquileia was not as busy as he had expected it to be, especially when compared with Constantinople. Few ships stood in the harbor, and many shops were closed.

At Paul's shop, Andreas found that the other merchant was a young man about five years older than he was. They made arrangements for Paul to go to the ship early the next morning to inspect the cargo and take it to his shop.

Then Paul offered to take Andreas to his uncle's farm, outside the city, to rest after the sea voyage. As they went through the city streets toward a gate, Andreas saw that many houses were in need of repair and even the city walls looked weak. Aquileia looked like a poverty-stricken city.

At the farm, many of the fields were barren and few workers could be seen. Andreas had heard about the problems in the Western Empire caused by the invasions of the barbarians and the weak government. Now he saw how the old way of life was crumbling away.

Later, Andreas talked to Paul and his uncle about the situation. The uncle explained that many workers and many landowners had left the area, frightened away by the fighting that always seemed to be going on. Paul and his uncle hoped that the Eastern Empire would come to the aid of the West and help it become a strong empire again.

6. After finishing
business in Aquileia,
Andreas and Paul went
on a trip to Pannonia
with another merchant.
There they did business
with a tribe
of Arian Visigoths,
and Andreas tried
to explain Catholic
Christianity to them.
Our imaginary story ends
as Andreas plans
to return to his home
in Constantinople.

A few days later, the cargo of Chinese cloth had been moved from the ship to Paul's shop, and payment had been made in money and goods. Andreas was now free to go home, but Paul had another idea. He was planning to go to Pannonia, which today we call Hungary, to sell goods to a Germanic people called Goths. Some of the Goths were still pagans, but many of the Visigoths, or west Goths, were Arian Christians. These were the barbarian people Paul planned to visit, and he suggested that Andreas go with him.

Andreas liked the idea of meeting a barbarian tribe of people who spoke a different language. He agreed to go, and the two young men set out together. The trip was long and difficult but at last they came to the Visigoths' encampment. Paul and Andreas were tense as they unrolled the cloth and spread out the other things Paul had for sale. The people crowding around seemed very barbarous and strange. They spoke a Germanic language that Paul and Andreas couldn't understand, and fearsome-looking weapons hung from their belts. But all went well, and the Visigothic leaders agreed with Paul on a price for his goods.

The Visigoths now seemed friendly, and Andreas began to explore the encampment to learn more about the Visigoths. He soon saw that they lived in tents and wagons and had very few utensils such as kettles, jars, and dishes. Their weapons, too, were simple, though they looked dangerous.

The Visigoths, Paul had told Andreas, were semi-nomads, which means that they traveled from place to place instead of living in a town. When they settled in a place, they farmed the land. Their farming methods were primitive, and after some time, the land was used up and would no longer grow crops. These people also killed all the game in the area they settled in. Then they moved on to find another place with good soil and game.

Andreas found a Visigoth who spoke a little Latin, a language Andreas had learned in school. He tried to find out why the Visigoths were Arian Christians rather than Catholic Christians. As Arians, the Visigoths believed that Jesus was an exceptional and special person, but they did not believe that he was God.

Andreas, using his oratory skills, tried to convince this Latin-speaking Visigoth that Catholic Christian beliefs were true. He reminded the Visigoth of Jesus' Baptism, during which a voice from heaven declared that Jesus was God's Son. But before Andreas could say much more, it was time for dinner. A fat ox had been roasting for hours, and now the visitors and the Visigoths gathered around to eat together. And the next day, Andreas would begin the trip across land and sea, to his home in Constantinople.

Our story about Andreas ends here. It has been an imaginary story, but it emphasizes some important ideas. In those long-ago days, in spite of danger, people continued to do business with each other. Ideas were exchanged along with money and goods. And at this time, the difference between the Eastern and Western Empires was growing greater. The East was prosperous and had a strong government, while in many places in the West, people became poorer and the old way of life disappeared as the barbarian tribes grew stronger.

7. Ambrose of Milan
was an important person
during this time, and
his words and deeds
helped the Church
grow stronger.

Ambrose began his career
as a governor, and
he ruled justly and kindly,
keeping the welfare
of the people in mind.

During the fourth century, barbarians began moving into the western part of the empire. Civil life and institutions were crumbling. Yet the Church of Jesus continued to grow, helped greatly by the example and guidance of people whose words and deeds proclaimed the gospel message. One such person was Ambrose, bishop of Milan.

Ambrose was born in 340 into a noble Christian family. His family lived in Trier, Italy, where his father was the praetorian prefect (governor) of Gaul. When his father died, Ambrose's mother returned to Rome with her three children. Marcellina, Ambrose's sister, dedicated her life to God. Today we would call her a nun. Ambrose and his brother went to school to learn grammar and rhetoric. When he finished school Ambrose entered the law courts, where he was able to use his gifts as a fine speaker and lawyer.

Thanks to his ability and his honesty, Ambrose attracted the attention of Petronius Probus, who was a very influential man in Rome. Petronius sent Ambrose to govern northern Italy. His headquarters would be the city of Milan. It is said that Petronius, who was a devout Christian, gave this advice to Ambrose: "When you get there, govern like a bishop rather than like a civil magistrate." Petronius meant that Ambrose should care for his people's welfare as well as for their obedience to law.

Ambrose himself believed that his first duty was to protect the lowly and the oppressed. He ruled in Milan with justice and mercy. He was well liked by the people, who often came to him for help and advice. Ambrose also tried to provide the public works and facilities which the city needed, such as water systems, schools, care for orphans and the sick. The welfare and prosperity of his people was always on his mind.

8. Ambrose was still
a catechumen—that is,
he was not yet baptized—
when the people of Milan
demanded that he become
their bishop.
Ambrose spent the rest
of his life serving
the Church. He preached
to his people and wrote
hymns and prayers
that began to be used
in other places, too.

While Ambrose was governor of Milan, the city had an Arian bishop named Auxentius. Milan was also a favorite residence of the Arian emperor Valentinian I. The influence of Arianism was strong. When Auxentius died, clergy and laity assembled in the local cathedral to choose a new bishop. The danger of a fight between Arians and Christians was very great. Ambrose went to the cathedral to calm things down and help the two sides reach an agreement.

Ambrose was greatly respected and admired as governor. When he entered the cathedral, according to one story, a little child cried out: "Ambrose bishop, Ambrose bishop!" The cry was taken up by others, and soon the assembly had made its choice. Ambrose had entered the cathedral as the civil governor. He left as the favored choice for bishop.

But Ambrose did not think himself fit for such an office. He was only a catechumen, and he had not even been baptized yet! He fled the city by night, but the next morning the people convinced him to return. They wanted him for their bishop, and so they made their wishes known to the emperor. Ambrose still wanted to get away, but both the people and the emperor approved of his election as bishop. Now certain that this was the will of God, Ambrose agreed to become bishop of Milan. He prepared to receive Baptism under the guidance of a priest named Simplicianus. He was baptized on November 30, 374. Within eight days he had received all the proper sacraments and had been consecrated a bishop.

Ambrose now studied the Bible devotedly. As a pastor, he was very eager to preach to his people and give them religious instruction. He made reforms in the liturgy and wrote some beautiful hymns that quickly spread to other dioceses in the West. His writings became an important treasury of practical religious thought for the Western Church. The Ambrosian rite used in Milan probably comes from a liturgy that Ambrose himself began.

Ambrose also had a new basilica built in Milan. When it was completed, a solemn procession was held. The relics of two martyrs — Gervasius and Protasius — were carried to the basilica and placed under the high altar.

9. Ambrose helped the Church
become more free
of the emperor's control.
Also, when the ruler
murdered many people,
Ambrose showed that
even the emperor
had to obey the laws
of the Church
and do penance
for his sin.

Shortly after Ambrose became bishop of Milan in 374, Gratian became emperor of the West. He was a Catholic Christian, but at this time there were still many pagans in the Roman Empire, including some noble families. The pagan religion was still legal, and the Roman government paid to support the temples and the priests.

Gratian changed this. In 382, he decreed that the government would no longer give money to the pagan religion. The pagan priests no longer had special privileges and the income from temple property was taken over by the government.

Up until this time, a statue of the goddess Victory had stood in the Roman Senate. Senators burned incense before it as they entered the Senate. This pagan statue in the Senate seemed to be a sign to the people that Rome was still a pagan empire.

Gratian had the statue taken away. This made the pagans very angry, and a year later Gratian was murdered. His son became emperor Valentinian II, but he was too young to rule. His mother, Empress Justina, ruled for him. The pagans worked through her to have the statue of the goddess put back. Just when

Justina seemed ready to agree, Ambrose spoke out strongly against it. His words were so vigorous and so wise that he won out. The goddess Victory was not put back into the Senate. And without the support of government money, the pagan religion continued to die out.

In 379, Theodosius became co-Augustus. He was a Catholic Christian, and at the beginning of his reign all pagan temples were closed for good. Sacrifices to the gods were forbidden, but pagans were not forced to become Christians.

In country places, people still clung to some of the old pagan rites, but the pagan religion was dead in the Roman Empire.

Though Ambrose and Theodosius were friends, Ambrose did not hesitate to defend the principles of the Church, even if he had to oppose the emperor himself. In 390, Theodosius ordered a terrible massacre of the people of Thessalonica. Theodosius was angry at the people there for killing some soldiers and the Gothic commander of the imperial garrison. Perhaps Theodosius feared that the Goths would make war if he did not punish the people of Thessalonica. So he had several thousand people killed.

When Ambrose heard about the massacre, he acted firmly. He excommunicated Theodosius and refused to offer the Eucharist when Theodosius was present. Ambrose ordered Theodosius to do public penance for his sin of murder. Theodosius was sorry for what he had done, and he stood outside the church door wearing a cloak of sackcloth and with ashes on his head, asking the faithful to pray for him. After eight months, Ambrose allowed him to take part in the Eucharist again. The message was clear: even an emperor had to obey God's laws and was subject to church authority in church affairs.

Nevertheless, there was real friendship between Theodosius and Ambrose. When Theodosius died, Bishop Ambrose composed a fine funeral sermon in his honor. Two years later, in 397, the great bishop himself died.

During Ambrose's years as bishop, the Church in the West had begun to express more clearly and firmly its freedom from the emperor's control. The Church was no longer willing to let rulers decide what Christians should believe. Ambrose himself was great and courageous. He would not let outside forces—such as emperors or the events of the time—decide what the Church should teach and do. He believed that the Holy Spirit was the true guide of the Church.

10. Another important person who lived at this time was Augustine. He was born in Africa in 354. As a young man, Augustine was not a baptized Christian, and he led a wild life. Monica, his mother, prayed for him daily. In 387, Augustine changed his way of life and was baptized by Bishop Ambrose.

Augustine, a great saint and a very important person in the history of the western Church, was born on November 15, 354. His home was Thagaste, a small African city not far from Carthage. Augustine's father, Patricius, was a pagan. His mother, Monica, was a devout Christian.

As a child, Augustine was enrolled as a catechumen, or a person who was studying the Christian faith, but he was not baptized. In those days, many parents did not have their children baptized, but had them study the faith so that they could join the Church as teenagers or young adults. Monica prayed constantly for her son, asking God to enlighten him.

Augustine had a good education, and as a young man he went to school in Carthage. There he led a wild life, he tells us in his writings. Also, he loved to study the great Latin writers, and he was inspired to seek truth in philosophy. He became a follower of Manichaeism, which was a blend of Christian and Persian ideas. It seemed to Augustine, and to many others, that this religion gave full and perfect knowledge. Augustine lived with a woman during this time, and they had a son, Adeodatus.

Augustine was now a teacher and he was offered a fine teaching job in Milan. He decided to leave the mother of his son and to become engaged to a wealthy woman. He traveled to Milan with Adeodatus, a friend named Alipius, and his mother, Monica.

In Milan, Augustine heard Ambrose preach, and this holy bishop made a great impression on Augustine. Under Ambrose's guidance, Augustine gave up Manichaeism. He began to study the Old Testament. Also, he learned about St. Antony and the monastic life.

One day, Augustine heard a child singing "Take up and read! Take up and read!" These were just the words of a children's song, but they seemed like a message to Augustine. He opened a book of Paul's letters and read these words: "Let us conduct ourselves becomingly . . . not in reveling and drunkenness, . . . not in quarreling and jealousy. But put on the Lord Jesus Christ." (Romans 13:13-14)

Augustine felt that these words were the answer to his searching. He gave up his career and the marriage he had planned. In April, 387, Ambrose baptized Augustine, his son Adeodatus, and his friend Alipius. From now on, Augustine would devote his life to the service of Christ and his Church.

11. A few years
after Augustine's Baptism,
Monica, his mother,
became ill and died.
Augustine then began
to lead a monastic life
in the country around
Hippo, a city in Africa.
In 391, Augustine
became a priest.

Augustine, his mother Monica, his son Adeodatus, and some friends decided to return to Africa, where Augustine owned some land. They planned to lead a monastic life and give themselves completely to God.

In the city of Ostia, a seaport near Rome, they waited for their ship to come. One day Monica said to Augustine, "Son, everything I have wanted in this world has been fulfilled, for you are now a Christian." Monica also said that now death would be happiness for her. Surprised, Augustine asked if she would not be afraid to be buried in Italy, so far away from her home in Africa.

Monica quickly replied, "I don't care where you bury me, but pray for me wherever you go. God is ever near, and he will find me on the day of judgment."

A few days later, Monica became very ill. She died in Ostia, and her grandson Adeodatus wept bitterly. Augustine, too, broke down and cried as he thought of his mother's care and love for him throughout his life.

Augustine and his companions traveled to Africa and arrived there in 388. Adeodatus died around this time. Augustine gave most of his worldly possessions to the poor. His group adopted a rule of life: prayer and medi-tation in common, frequent fasting, and similar practices. Augustine also finished writing several works that he had begun in Milan. His rule of life won many followers, and more than thirty monasteries in Africa were based on it before his own death.

Augustine did not neglect work of charity. He became very well known and many people came to him for help. One day, Augustine went to Hippo to visit a sick friend, and he took part in a church service there. The people recognized him, seized him, and took him to the bishop. They asked that he be ordained a priest. Augustine agreed, and he became a priest in 391.

12. Augustine became
bishop of Hippo
in 395. As bishop,
he preached to his people
every day. He spoke out
against the Donatists,
who taught that
sacraments were not valid
if the priest were in sin.
Augustine taught that
the holiness
of the sacraments
came from Jesus
and did not depend
on the priest.

In 395, four years after Augustine was ordained a priest, he was made the bishop of Hippo. He carried out his duties with energy and dedication. He preached every day, sometimes more than once a day, because he felt that preaching was the duty of every bishop.

As bishop, he had to argue against a view that threatened to divide the Church. It was the view of Donatus, bishop of Carthage, who had established a church of his own. His followers were called Donatists. Donatus had started to preach a view that did not agree with church tradition. He maintained that the Church should be a community of people who made no mistakes and committed no sins. Sacraments administered by sinful priests were not valid, said Donatus. For example, according to Donatus, if a sinful priest baptized a person, that person would not have received the sacrament of Baptism.

Augustine felt he had a duty to argue against this view, which was called a heresy. He argued against it point by point. His basic argument was that the visible Church was a means of salvation even if some of the Church's ministers were unworthy people. The Church was holy, Augustine said, because Jesus made it holy, and the sacraments were effective because Jesus gave them force.

If the effectiveness of the sacraments depended on the holiness of the priest who administered them, then people's trust and hope would lie in a human being. Augustine maintained that the holiness of the priestly minister did not increase or decrease the sacredness of a sacrament. Real hope of salvation lay in Jesus, Augustine said, and in the presence of the Holy Spirit whom Jesus had given to his Church.

Augustine's argument with the Donatist view helped all Christians to form a clearer idea of the nature of the Church, its dependence on Jesus, and the true relationship between a sacrament and its minister.

During his years as bishop, Augustine never failed to carry out works of charity or to teach his people more about the faith. He showed great concern for ordinary people and their problems. He also thought about his own life and how good God had been to him. He wrote a famous book called *Confessions*, expressing sorrow for his early wrongdoing and praising God for giving him grace. This story of Augustine's own life is one of the great classics of western culture.

13. Germanic tribes from
    beyond the Roman frontiers
    began to move
    into imperial territory.
    They took over the land
    and looted cities.
    Even the city of Rome
    was looted in 410.
    The Western Empire
    began to break up
    into small, local sections.
    The Church faced the
    problem of converting
    the new people.

Germanic tribes had long occupied the forests and marshlands of northern and central Europe. Hunger for food, need for more land, and fear of other tribes began to drive these Germanic people across the frontiers of the Roman Empire. In return for being allowed to live inside the empire, they promised to defend the imperial territory from outside invaders. Along the Rhine River in Gaul, for example, German-speaking Franks settled and guarded the Roman frontier.

On the night of December 31, 406, the Rhine River was frozen over. Tribes of Vandals, Alans, and Suevis crossed on the ice and marched into Gaul, defeating the Franks who were supposed to stop them.

The invading Germanic tribes drove through Gaul, causing devastation everywhere. Only Toulouse, under the direction of its bishop, managed to defend itself successfully against them. In 408-409, three tribes crossed the

Pyrenees and entered Spain. The Vandals eventually swept through Spain and crossed over to Africa. There they conquered the weakly defended provinces, which offered rich supplies of grain and wealthy cities.

Meanwhile, the Visigoths had invaded the empire. They were repulsed by the emperor's army at Constantinople, and turned westward, into Italy. In 410, under their leader Alaric, they invaded Rome and looted or sacked it, carrying away gold, silver, and many precious things.

These barbarian invasions had serious and important results for both the Church and the empire. The invasions affected the western part of the empire and helped to create a feeling of separation between it and the eastern part of the empire. The Eastern Empire escaped attack, and its cities were not looted. After the invasions, Emperor Theodosius II, who lived in Constantinople, offered to make treaties with the invading peoples in the Western Empire. Most of them settled in the empire as allies.

The new tribes followed their own customs and traditions rather than Roman law. Each tribe or group of tribes wanted to rule in its own way, and so the Western Empire began to dissolve into local sections. Soon big differences began to show up between East and West in lifestyle, customs, and ways of making a living. In the West, the civilization of the ancient world was passing away.

The arrival of the barbarians also had important consequences for the Church. Some tribes followed their old pagan traditions. Many, however, had become familiar with Christianity, and they had adopted the heretical Arian form of Christianity. Thus they brought the problem of Arianism into the West, and they clung to it fiercely. The Catholic Church in the West faced the task of preaching the correct faith to the new arrivals and their descendants.

14. Pelagius, a British monk,
fled from Rome in 410
when the barbarians
invaded the city.
He went to Africa
and spread his teachings.
Pelagius taught that
children need not
be baptized and that
other sacraments and
prayers were not
of first importance.
Augustine spoke out
firmly against Pelagius's
teachings.

In the fifth century another view threatened the Christian faith: Pelagianism. Its founder, Pelagius, was a British monk who went to Rome around 390. There he lived a strict life of Christian asceticism without attaching himself closely to any community of monks. He won many admirers because of his speaking ability and his commitment to the highest Christian ideals. Pelagius wanted people to live a very strict moral life, and he overestimated the ability of human beings to live good lives without receiving God's help through the sacraments.

When the Visigoths invaded Rome in 410, Pelagius took refuge in Africa. His views, thanks mainly to the work of his disciple Coelestius, soon spread widely among the people in Augustine's area. Augustine reacted very strongly against Pelagius's idea of original sin. Pelagius claimed original sin was a personal sin, belonging only to Adam himself, and so it did not affect other human beings. For this reason, he claimed, there was no need to baptize infants. Pelagius also considered the other sacraments and prayer to be of secondary importance. The most important thing, according to Pelagius, was to lead a very strict moral life. Pelagius went so far as to urge all Christians to live lives of complete poverty and not to get married.

Augustine, on the other hand, insisted that all human beings were members of one human family, and therefore Adam's sin affected everyone. Even newborn babies were part of a humanity in need of God's salvation, so their Baptism was of the greatest importance. Augustine also argued against Pelagius's notion that human beings could attain the divine life of grace through their own efforts. To Pelagius, Jesus was merely a good example for people to follow. This view meant that Jesus' passion, death, and resurrection had no meaning because each person could work out his or her own salvation.

Augustine insisted that it is God's freely given love that saves us. Through the Church we receive God's loving grace which gives us the strength to fight evil, pardons us when we sin, and enables us to find the right road again. Moreover, said Augustine, the Church does not demand complete poverty and virginity of all its members; nor does the Church expect people to be completely without fault. Instead, people must be sincerely willing to follow Christ in the Church, choosing whatever path in life God points out to them.

15. Augustine wrote an important book showing a Christian view of history. In this book, called *The City of God,* he described two cities—one good and one evil. The cities were mixed together and would be until the end of human life on earth.

Augustine wrote an important Christian explanation of history entitled *The City of God.* It was the finest defense of Christianity against outside criticism which had been written up to that time. It was also the most important attempt that had been made to explain all of human history in Christian terms. This book has continued to be a major influence on Christian thought.

Augustine wrote this work because Christians were often blamed for the misfortunes that were now befalling the Roman Empire. This accusation was being made again after Alaric and his Visigoths sacked Rome. From 413 to 426 Augustine worked on *The City of God,* his major defense of Christianity. In the first part he showed that idol worship did not ensure happiness either in this world or the next. In the second part Augustine described two cities: the city of God and the earthly city. Good people were citizens of the city of God; bad people were citizens of the earthly city. Until the end of history the two cities could not be clearly marked off from one another. They would be mixed together so that only God could tell them apart.

Even the Church could not be equated with the city of God. The earthly city might be part of the Church, so Christians had to be on the lookout. Good and bad people lived inside the Church, and that would continue until the day of judgment. Good people and good deeds might also be in places where one might expect only evil and the earthly city. Only at the end of time and the last judgment would the two cities be clearly separated.

Augustine had already expressed many of these ideas in his sermons and other writings. But in *The City of God* he spelled them out fully.

16. In 430, Vandals attacked
the city of Hippo.
Bishop Augustine,
now very old, died
before the city fell.
At the time of his death,
the ancient civilizations
of Greece and Rome
were coming to an end
as the invading barbarians
began to take power.
Augustine, in his writings,
left the Church
a reminder to have faith
in God's help and love.

Augustine realized that because of the barbarian conquests, his native Africa would soon be cut off from the Roman Empire. He suffered greatly because he deeply admired the cultural traditions of Rome. In 430 his city of Hippo was attacked by the Vandals. Augustine, now in his seventies, was still hard at work, but he also felt a strong longing to be united with God. He prayed that the city of Hippo might be saved from the assault of the Vandals. If the Vandals were victorious, he hoped that God would give people the strength to accept what had been his will. But Augustine himself longed to be called home to God, and his longing was fulfilled. He grew ill during the third month of the siege and died after ten days. The feast of this great Christian is celebrated on August 28.

As the ancient civilization of Greece and Rome came to an end, this great person left a message for all future generations. Augustine summed up his wholehearted search for God when he said, "Our hearts are restless, God, until they rest in you." Augustine emphasized the importance of the Church, insisting that salvation did not depend on the goodness of human beings or on their efforts alone but on the will of Jesus. The Church needed the collaboration of human beings, he said, but it also could rely on the grace of God to carry out its work of bringing human beings to salvation.

17. During the time
of Augustine and Ambrose,
a man named Jerome
did very important work
for the Church.
He is remembered especially
for translating the Bible,
which he did with the help
of two women, Paola
and Eustochium.

Jerome was another important person who lived about the same time as Ambrose and Augustine. He was born into a Christian family in Stridon, a border area near the city of Aquileia around the year 342. Jerome's family wanted him to have a very good education, so he was sent to study grammar in Rome. There he began to put together an excellent library. Books were his faithful companions throughout his life.

When he left Rome, Jerome traveled in Gaul until he decided to adopt the strict life of a religious hermit. He withdrew to a desert area on the Syrian frontier for five years. There he led a strict life and began to study Hebrew, the original language of the Old Testament. Jerome then went to Antioch and was ordained a priest. He moved on to Constantinople, became a friend of Gregory Nanzianzus, and began his long career of writing books.

Pope Damasus I asked Jerome to serve as his secretary in Rome. In 385, after three years on the job, Jerome was heartily sick of high society and Roman nobles. So when Pope Damasus died, Jerome went on pilgrimage through the monasteries of Palestine and Egypt. He was accompanied by two Roman noblewomen, Paola and her daughter Eustochium, who had been impressed by his strong personality and deep religious convictions. In Bethlehem they founded two monasteries which shared a common church. One was a community for men under the direction of Jerome; the other was a community for women under the direction of Paola. Jerome had brought his books along, and he spent his last years in serious study, writing, and prayerful meditation.

Jerome wrote many books and letters. His most important work was his translation into Latin of the Old and New Testaments of the Bible, which were originally written in Hebrew and Greek. In this work, he was helped greatly by Paola and Eustochium.

Jerome translated the Bible into Latin because at that time Latin was the common language for educated people. No matter what language they spoke in their daily lives, people learned to read and write in Latin.

Jerome's translation was called *The Vulgate,* from the Latin word *vulgaris* which means "of the common people," because it could be generally used by educated people. The Vulgate took the place of earlier translations and for many centuries was widely used in the Western Church.

18. Early in the fifth century,
a dispute arose about Mary.
Some Christians thought
that she should be called
Mother of God
because Jesus was God.
Others thought that Mary
should be called only
Mother of Jesus
because he was also man.
At the Council of Ephesus,
the Church taught
that Mary was
Mother of God.

Another dispute arose among Christians in Constantinople around 428. Should Mary be called the Mother of God, since Jesus was God? Or should she simply be called the Mother of a human being named Jesus, since Jesus was also a human being? The bishop of Constantinople, Nestorius, proclaimed the second view. He said that Mary was not the Mother of God but only the Mother of Jesus the human being. Those who believed that Nestorius was right were called Nestorians.

Cyril, the bishop of Alexandria, strongly opposed Nestorius's view. He explained that if Mary was only the Mother of the human Jesus, then Jesus would be two persons, one human, one divine.

In 430, Pope Celestine I decided to settle the matter. He told Nestorius and his congregation that Mary was to be considered the Mother of God. He ordered Nestorius to give up his opinion.

Nestorius stuck to his ideas and continued to spread this doctrine. Theodosius II decided to call a council of eastern bishops to settle the issue. The Council opened in the main church of Ephesus in June, 431. The Creed approved at the Councils of Nicaea and Constantinople— the one still used today— was read. Then the Council considered the writings of Cyril and Nestorius, and their replies to each other. A letter from the pope to the bishop of Constantinople was also read.

One by one the bishops voted in favor of Cyril's view, rejecting the ideas of Nestorius as serious errors. It took only one day for them to declare that Mary was the Mother of God. Nestorianism was declared by the Church to be a heresy. Nestorius was stripped of his rank as bishop and of his right to perform priestly functions.

The people of Ephesus had particular devotion to Mary and eagerly awaited the results of the Council. When the bishops came out in the evening with their decision, the people welcomed them with a torchlight procession. They went through the streets singing hymns in honor of Jesus and Mary. The Church had officially proclaimed Mary *theotokos,* the Mother of God.

19. Soon after the
Council of Ephesus,
the Monophysite belief
began to spread.
Monophysites believed
that Jesus was truly God
but not truly human.
At the Council
of Chalcedon in 451,
the Church taught that
Jesus had two natures,
one divine and one human.
Together they formed
a single person.

After the Council of Ephesus in 431, a controversial belief began to spread. It was taught by a monk named Eutyches, who claimed in his writings that the divine nature in Jesus more or less took over and absorbed his human nature. Thus, according to this theory, Jesus had only one nature (*monophysis* in Greek), a divine one. People who held this view were called *Monophysites.*

The eastern bishops met in Constantinople in 448 to discuss Monophysitism. They concluded that Jesus was both God and a human being, that he had both a divine nature and a human nature. Eutyches was condemned as a heretic.

Eutyches, however, had strong influence on the emperor. He persuaded Theodosius II to call a new Council, which met in Ephesus in 449. Pope Leo I sent representatives with letters which contained the Church's doctrine. The letters were to be read at the sessions. Theodosius, however, prevented this and disregarded Rome's views. He stationed

soldiers around the Council members to frighten them as they voted. As a result, they voted to reinstate Eutyches.

When Pope Leo I heard what had happened, he was very angry. He wrote sternly to the emperor, demanding that he annul the decisions of the Council. When Theodosius died as a result of an accident, he was succeeded by Marcian. The new emperor favored the pope's wishes and called a new Council which took place in Chalcedon in 451. After many lively sessions the bishops at the Council went along with the pope's view. They solemnly proclaimed: "Our Lord Jesus Christ is of the same substance as the Father in his divinity, and of the same substance as us in his humanity. He became like us in all things, except for sin. The difference between his two natures is not eliminated by their union. Each nature retains its own particular features; together they form one single person."

20. The primacy of the pope
now began to be stressed.
Innocent I and
Leo the Great are
two popes who
emphasized this idea.

The primacy of the pope— that is, the authority of the bishop of Rome over other bishops— began to be stressed more and more during this period.

Innocent I was pope from 402 to 417. He declared that the pope was the head and leader of all the bishops. He had the power to judge other bishops and to settle disputes between them. Innocent I urged his fellow

bishops to submit important cases to him. He was also concerned that the Eastern Church remain faithful and obedient to Rome. The division of the Roman Empire and the distance between Rome in the West and Constantinople in the East had weakened the ties between the two sections of the Church.

Leo I, also known as Leo the Great, was pope from 440 to 461. He was one of the first popes to claim systematically that Jesus Christ, the one eternal bishop or overseer of the Church, had delegated his power to the bishop of Rome. That is, Leo said that Jesus wished the bishop of Rome to have primacy as pope.

Leo used his power mainly to preserve the Church's accepted doctrine. For example, he took action against Monophysitism by calling the Council of Chalcedon. Local bishops and churches appealed to him to settle doubtful cases, and he wrote many words of instruction, counsel, and correction. Leo felt that the pope had the obligation to serve others. Christ had said that among his followers, the leaders must be the most dedicated servants of all.

21. Leo the Great
was a courageous pope.
He tried to safeguard
Christian doctrine,
even if he had to oppose
the emperor.
He also defended
the people of Rome
against the attack
of Attila the Hun.

Pope Leo I did not hesitate to criticize Emperor Theodosius II when he thought that the correct Christian doctrine was in danger. Perhaps no pope before him had displayed such a lofty sense of mission and responsibility in caring for God's people. Leo's letters and sermons, which are highly valued by historians, reflect the many aspects of his personality and his concerns. A man of great character and courage, he truly deserved to be called Leo the Great.

Besides working to safeguard Christian doctrine, Pope Leo was not afraid to confront

external political dangers. In the middle of the fifth century, Attila and his Huns were causing destruction and death in Europe. They had swept across Europe from the Balkans and the eastern parts of the empire. In Gaul, an army of Visigoths, Franks, Burgundians, and Romans finally stopped the westward advance of the Huns. Attila then moved into northern Italy, where his forces struck terror among the people. The inhabitants of Aquileia, a rich and prosperous city, left their homes in fear of Attila and took refuge on the islands of a lagoon in the Gulf of Venice. Thus began the famous city of Venice.

Pope Leo, well aware of Attila's advance, wanted to spare the rest of Italy from the invaders. In 452 he went out to meet Attila, armed only with his courage and his wisdom as a statesman. Yet the unarmed pope managed to convince Attila to withdraw his army and spare the city of Rome from attack. Three years later, in 455, Leo could not prevent Genseric and his Vandals from sacking Rome, but he did persuade them not to slaughter the inhabitants.

22. Christianity was brought to Britain during the centuries it was occupied by the Romans. When the Roman officials left, the Church in Britain was strong and growing.

Christianity came to southern England through the Romans, who established forts and colonies on the island. When Christianity became the favored religion in the Roman Empire, it grew rapidly in England. There were several bishops in England by the first half of the fourth century.

Christianity took root mainly in the fortified towns where most imperial officials and Romans lived. There Latin, the language of Rome, was spoken. There, too, could be found some pagan temples, because part of the population remained loyal to their local religions. Paganism was even more widespread in rural areas outside the towns, where Christianity was slow to spread.

We know that by the end of the fourth century the members of the Church in England were discussing certain religious issues and problems. Some bishops crossed over from Gaul to help their fellow Christians settle conflicts. The missionary spirit was also alive in the English Church. Around 400 Ninian went to preach the Gospel to the Picts in what is now called Scotland. The area lay outside Roman control and was divided into tribal kingdoms.

At the same time Christianity was spreading in Britain, Roman officials and soldiers began leaving England and making their way back toward Rome. The Roman Empire had lost its power and could no longer hold or defend England. Soon Germanic tribes invaded the island. In 314, London and York —already episcopal cities—had seen the arrival of the Angles, Jutes, and Saxons.

This period of about 200 years was a time of shocking change for local peoples, who belonged to Celtic-speaking tribes. As the Romans left, these people would find unity in a common faith— Christianity. The essential elements of the Christian faith would mingle with various local customs and practices. Tribal kingdoms would again crop up in southern England, but the Christian faith and traces of Roman culture would also take root. Monasticism would win great favor among the Celts, and courageous, individualistic monks would leave their mark on Great Britain, Ireland, and the European continent.

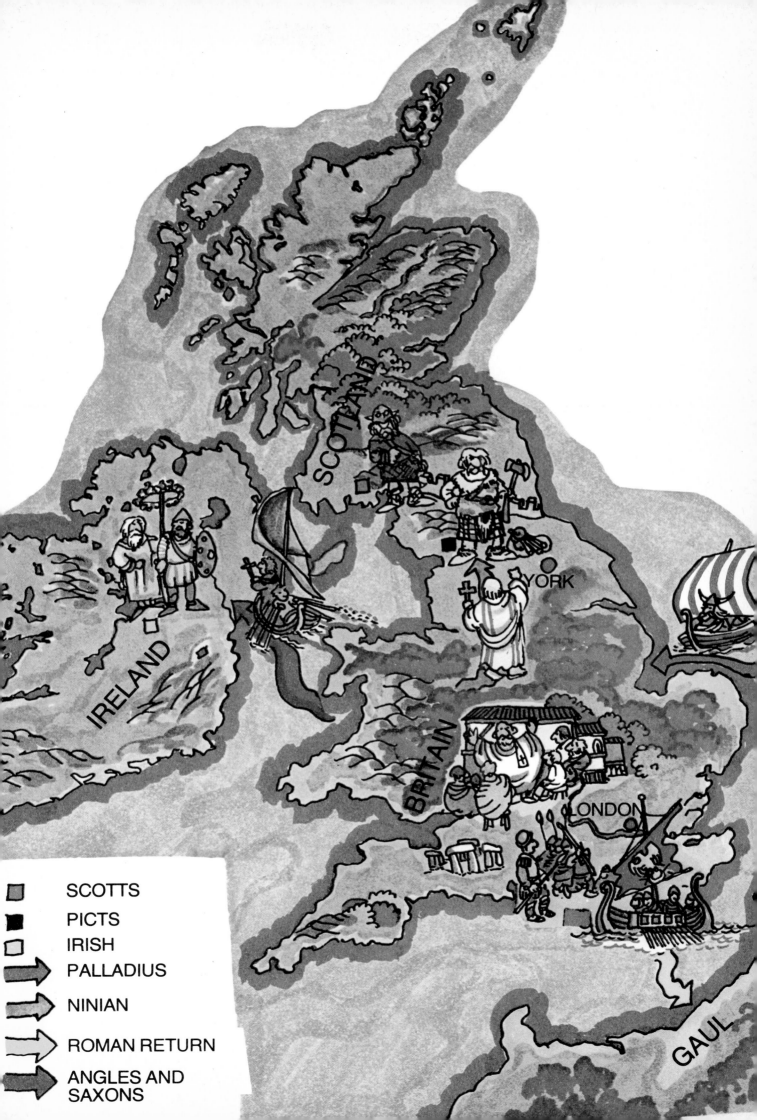

SCOTLAND

IRELAND

YORK

BRITAIN

LONDON

GAUL

SCOTTS

PICTS

IRISH

PALLADIUS

NINIAN

ROMAN RETURN

ANGLES AND
SAXONS

23. Ireland became Christian in the fifth century, due to the work of Patrick, the Apostle of Ireland.

Ireland, the island lying west of Britain, now came under the influence of Christianity. The Celts in Ireland around the year 400 were divided into five main tribal kingdoms known as *tuathas*. In 431 the first bishop, Palladius, was sent to the island. He died shortly after the arrival of Patrick, who is considered the real Apostle of Ireland.

Patrick wrote an account of some of the details of his life, and, in time, many legendary details were added. It seems that he was born in England. At the age of sixteen he was captured by pirates, who took him to Ireland as a slave. There, herding sheep, he spent much time alone and turned to God. After six years he managed to escape and found his way home. He studied in Gaul, became a priest, accepted the monastic way of life, and was consecrated a bishop. He himself tells us that he was called in a dream to go back to Ireland. There he carried on with astonishing success the work begun by Palladius.

Patrick won many converts among both simple people and tribal leaders. He traveled over the countryside by chariot or cart. Sometimes his life was in danger. One reason for his success seems to have been that he tackled his work clan by clan. Later, clan boundaries became the basis of episcopal dioceses.

The monastic spirit appealed to the Irish, and monasteries sprang up quickly. They became centers of ascetic living, of apostolic work among the people, and of highly advanced learning for that time. First, the abbot-bishops and monks tackled the work of making Ireland completely Christian. Then they moved out to leave their mark as apostles and scholars on western Europe. Patrick's fine work in Ireland would endure and help spread the Gospel to other areas.

24. The Roman Empire became weaker and weaker as barbarian tribes took over imperial territory. In 476, the last Roman ruler was deposed, and the Roman Empire in the West came to an end.

By the middle of the fifth century, the Roman Empire in the West was becoming weaker and could not enforce its laws.

One cause of trouble was the activity of various Germanic tribes. Some of them had made treaties with the emperor, but many disregarded the treaties and continued to fight and to take over more territory. The imperial army in the West did not establish peace, and often its soldiers were barbarians themselves. Imperial officials in Constantinople often sent one or more tribes of barbarians to fight against another invading group of barbarians. Officials in Ravenna, which had now become the capital of the empire in the West instead of Milan, used the same tactics.

When Genseric and his Vandals crossed over from Africa and sacked Rome in 455, they also captured Sicily and Sardinia. These were the last sources of grain supplies for the imperial cities of Italy. Food became scarce.

In addition, many people in the West did not feel loyal to the Roman Empire. To maintain the frontiers, emperors had imposed heavy taxes on the citizens. Even those who farmed their own land in the country felt the weight of growing taxes. Many left their farms and fled to the cities. Others went to lands under control of the Germanic tribes, where imperial tax officials could not reach them. Sometimes the peasants rose in revolt against imperial officials who tried to collect taxes, farm products, or other fees.

Commerce, trade, and other economic activities in the West declined just as farming did. Landowners and wealthy citizens often thought only about their own interests and did all they could to avoid taxes.

In general, the authority of the emperor now meant little in the West. The western emperor was often a mere puppet under the control of one barbarian leader or another. In 476 the ruler in Ravenna refused to give land to members of the barbarian army. Odoacer, the barbarian leader, took over the city and deposed Romulus Augustulus, the last person to have a claim to the imperial throne. Thus the year 476 marks what is called the end of the Roman Empire in the West. The Roman Empire in the East, also known as the Byzantine Empire, would continue for another thousand years.

25. Without the central
Roman government,
various national groups
in the former empire
began to follow
their own ways of life.
Farm life, especially,
was reorganized.
The influence
of Christianity
was important.

The invasion of the barbarians, the decline of imperial rule, and the spread of Christianity had important effects on the social and economic life of the various peoples who had been living in the empire.

Since the Roman Empire had covered such a vast amount of territory, it included peoples with very different traditions, customs, and languages. For example, there were Celts and Iberians in Spain, Celts in Britain and Gaul, Celts and Ligurians in parts of Italy, and the Illyrians in the Balkans. The distinctive traditions of these various peoples had been somewhat covered over by Roman forms of government and administration when the Roman Empire was strong. Now native ways of thinking and doing things surfaced once again, helping to shape social life somewhat differently.

One example of this was the reorganization of farm life. The Roman nobility in the countryside had organized farming around the villa. In a villa, several buildings were in the center of a group of fields. An official or landowner lived at the villa with his family and his servants. The official directed the farm work and gathered the harvest produced by his slaves and farm workers, known as *coloni*. In theory the coloni were supposed to be free settlers who received a plot of land in return for services and farm products. The villa system had provided the Roman overlords and their supporters with food supplies and wealth when the system was working.

Now native clans and barbarian tribes began to take over the land. They preferred to gather in small villages where several families or groups occupied the land. They built their houses as they had before the villa system became widespread. Tribal leaders and tribal councils took charge of social life as the villas and their network of activity began to disappear.

Christian ideas also began to change the practice of slavery. Church leaders encouraged slave owners to turn their slaves into free people. The flight of people from imperial territory also prompted farm owners to invite free settlers to work their land. But the standard of living of these free settlers, or coloni, was often no better than that of slaves. Compared to life today, life in these times was very difficult.

26. Arian Vandals in Africa persecuted Catholic Christians and tried to destroy the Church. The African Church was brave under this persecution. Outstanding was Bishop Fulgentius, who continued to preach the gospel message from exile.

During Augustine's lifetime it seemed that the African Church would flourish and enjoy peace for awhile. Then in 429 Genseric and his Vandals crossed into Africa from Spain, invading Tangiers and also Hippo. It would mean oppression and persecution for the Christians of North Africa. The Vandals had become Arians, and they were hostile to the Catholic Church. They persecuted church leaders in particular. Many Christians began to flee when the Vandals arrived. Until he died, Augustine urged the clergy to stay wherever a community of Christians remained.

The Vandals, however, were savage invaders and persecutors. They burned churches, looted monasteries, and sacked homes. The

streets were crowded with people desperately trying to flee from the invaders. Some bishops were tortured to death; others were chased out. Some Christians were killed for refusing to accept Arianism; others gave in. It was impossible to carry on any real pastoral work. Just when it seemed that things might grow more peaceful, a new wave of persecution would break out. In 483 many exiled Christians endured a terrible march into the desert, where they died.

Around the year 505, the Catholic Church was finally left in peace for awhile, and several new bishops were appointed. Then Thrasamund, the Vandal ruler, issued a decree in 507 exiling both newly-consecrated bishops and the ones who had consecrated them. Among the exiled bishops was the recently appointed bishop of Ruspe named Fulgentius. He moved to Sardinia, where he established a monastery. He took charge of the monastic community and engaged in preaching. He seems to have been a good theologian and wrote several excellent summaries of Catholic doctrine. He also wrote many letters to maintain contact with other exiled bishops and the Christian communities of North Africa.

Fulgentius's reputation and authority grew so much that Thrasamund himself asked Fulgentius to come back to Carthage.

He wanted Fulgentius to act as judge in an argument that had arisen between Catholics and Arians. Once back in Africa, however, Fulgentius took advantage of the opportunity to preach the gospel message and give support to the Church. Thrasamund regretted the freedom he had promised Fulgentius, and sent him into exile once again. Fulgentius symbolized the courage of the North African Church. It tried to carry out its mission under the harsh rule of the Vandals.

27. Clovis, a pagan king,
united Gaul under his rule
in 486. Later he became
a Catholic Christian,
and many Franks
followed his lead.
Close ties soon formed
between the Church
and the Franks.

The Franks were one of the first tribes to settle within the boundaries of the Roman Empire. For a long time they had been recognized allies of the Romans, though they had little liking for Roman culture. They also kept their pagan religion, even after many other Germanic tribes had accepted the Arian version of Christianity.

The Franks occupied the northern part of present-day France, then called Gaul, and they were divided into many small kingdoms. Great changes took place when a young and energetic man named Clovis became king of one group of Franks in 481. He put an end to Roman rule in Gaul in 486 and continued to move southward, pushing back the Visigoths—one of the Gothic tribes—as he went along. By the end of his career, Clovis had

taken over most of Gaul, united all the Franks under his rule, and won the Franks to Catholic Christianity by his own acceptance of Baptism. Clovis used both good and bad methods to accomplish his aims. Historians have judged him in many different ways. Some even describe him as a brilliant and forceful gangster who knew how to do the right thing at the right time.

There is no doubt about the fact that Clovis was baptized as a Catholic Christian, and that this event had enormous influence on later European history. Clovis was originally a pagan. He married a young Burgundian princess, Clotilda, as part of his plan to extend his rule into Burgundy. Clotilda was a Catholic, and she persuaded Clovis to let their sons be baptized. Later on Clovis found himself in a fierce battle with the Alemanni tribe. According to Gregory of Tours, who wrote *History of the Franks*, Clovis vowed that he would become a Christian if he won the battle. He won, and somewhere between 496 and 498 he and many of his followers were baptized in Rheims. Many other Franks soon followed his example.

This was the first time a pagan Germanic people had adopted the Catholic faith instead of Arianism. Close ties soon developed between the Church and the Franks. Together they would spread Catholic Christianity to many other parts of Europe, and their alliance would pave the way for the empire of Charlemagne several centuries later.

28. Catholic Christianity
spread rapidly in France,
Germany, and Belgium.
At first, priests
and bishops for the Franks
had to come from other
lands. After some time,
Franks began to have
their own priests.
Later, Frankish bishops
began to serve the Church.

Catholic Christianity now began to spread rapidly in the Frankish lands in the areas now known as France, Germany, and Belgium. When a new Christian community was formed through the efforts of missionaries, it usually was supported for some time by the local church which had sent the missionaries. Often the supporting church provided priests to celebrate Mass and perform other church services. Just as a young child must look to its parents for support, so new communities of Christians had to look to established church communities for support at first. Before 600 the Frankish churches needed priests, bishops, and missionaries from elsewhere.

Soon the new communities began to ordain priests of their own. It was more difficult to find men qualified to serve as bishops, however, so bishops continued to come from other areas with a longer Christian heritage. Around 550 the bishops of Maastricht, Cologne, Mainz, and Strassburg came largely from Aquitaine, in southwest France. Not until around 600 did native priests begin to be selected as bishops in Frankish churches.

The whole region had suffered a great deal during the barbarian invasions. Now having a local clergy insured a better future for the Church in the region.

29. Around the year 500,
in the country
today called France,
a bishop named Caesar
led the diocese of Arles.
Caesar emphasized
the importance of God's
grace. He continually
preached the Gospel
to his people.

Around 470 a man who would be an out-standing bishop was born in eastern France. His name was Caesar. When he was twenty, Caesar completed his studies for the priest-hood in the famous monastery on the island of Lerins in the Mediterranean. He was or-dained a priest and served as the father superior of a monastery.

In 503, Caesar was appointed bishop of Arles. At the time, Arles was a big town in southern Gaul and its diocese was one of the most important in the West. Under Caesar's leadership, Arles took first place among the dioceses of Gaul and Spain. In 513 Caesar went to visit Pope Symmachus in Rome. The pope had such confidence in Caesar that he appointed Caesar as his vicar or representa-tive in southern France and Spain. Caesar was the first bishop in the West to receive the pallium, a circular band which bishops wear around the neck on special occasions. The pallium is conferred by the pope. Before this, only the pope had worn the pallium in the West.

Until his death in 542, Caesar of Arles de-voted his efforts as a bishop to three main tasks. He tried to combat mistaken doctrines, to preach the gospel message, and to organize monasteries.

In confronting mistaken doctrines, Caesar tried to help people understand the connec-tion between God's grace and the free will of human beings. God's grace was necessary for human beings, he said, not only to begin good deeds but also to finish them. Since human

beings enjoyed free will, they could freely decide to follow Christ and do what was right, or they could reject Christ and do what was wrong.

Caesar wrote two rules to help organize monastic life. One set of rules was for monasteries of men, the other for monasteries of women. The influence of Augustine can be seen in the rules Caesar drew up. These rules were followed by later organizers of monasteries.

Caesar often preached to his people. His homilies were simple and clear, since they were addressed to plain, uneducated people. At that time, people still took part in many magical practices which were left over from pagan days. Caesar argued against believing in magic and urged his people to practice charity and almsgiving. He told them to think about their actions and to do penance. In order to avoid sin, he said, they should think about Jesus during their daily lives.

30. Theodoric, an Arian Ostrogoth, became ruler of what had been the Western Roman Empire. His capital city was Ravenna. Theodoric was a strong, capable ruler.

The various tribes of Goths were important in shaping the new world that developed out of the ruins of the Western Roman Empire. They possessed military ability, and some of their leaders were fine organizers and rulers. The kingdoms which the Goths carved out of the old imperial territory in the West would have great influence there for awhile.

One tribe or group of Goths was known as the Ostrogoths, or East Goths. After living for some time on the Russian steppes, they moved westward into Pannonia, which was under the rule of the Byzantine emperor. The eastern emperors could have fought the Ostrogoths, but made them allies instead, and used them to carry out their plans in the West. Though barbarians had invaded the West, the eastern emperors still regarded themselves as the legitimate rulers and wanted to exercise real control over the West once again.

Theodoric, an Ostrogoth, went to Constantinople as a hostage-ally at the age of seven. He lived at the Byzantine court for eleven years and married a princess of the imperial household. In 476 Emperor Zeno gave Theodoric the title *patrician*, which means "protector of the Romans." Later, Zeno sent Theodoric to take back Italy from Odoacer. This was an important mission. Theodoric, hoping to establish his own kingdom, eagerly accepted the assignment.

In 490 Theodoric and his troops arrived in Italy and successfully fought the armies of Odoacer. Defeated on several occasions, Odoacer decided to retreat to his capital, Ravenna. Theodoric managed to besiege and conquer Ravenna, luring Odoacer into a trap and killing him by deceit.

Theodoric now began to act as an independent ruler, even though he recognized the authority of the eastern emperor and acted as his representative. Ravenna became the capital of an Ostrogothic kingdom ranging from Italy to Arles, in Gaul. The kingdom included the old capital city of Rome. Theodoric himself was strongly attracted to Roman culture and the imperial tradition. He wanted to rebuild Roman civilization on the basis of an intermingling between Goths and Romans. He tried to respect the traditional Roman institutions of government to some extent. He left the Roman Senate in operation and did not expel Italians, but the rule of the Senate was now restricted to the city of Rome. Theodoric's court in Ravenna was modeled on that of the Roman emperor, and there too Italians played important roles. Theodoric stood out as an extremely able ruler in an age of general disorder. Though his tribe was Arian, he seems to have had little effect—good or bad—on the growth of the Church.

31. While Theodoric ruled
in the West,
relations between
the Arian Ostrogoths
and Catholic Italians
were mostly peaceful.
Theodoric made Ravenna,
his capital city.
Theodoric's reign
was an important step
in the change
from the ancient world
to the Middle Ages.

During most of Theodoric's reign, the conquering Ostrogoths and their subjects lived together peacefully. Ravenna was now the capital city. From it a new spirit of prosperity and revival spread over Italy. The revival affected culture, the arts, and even religion. Theodoric wanted Ravenna to become the center of Arian religious worship in Italy. This was an important stage in the movement from the older world of classical tradition to the later world of the Middle Ages.

Building went on at a rapid pace. Ravenna took on a distinctive look during the Ostrogothic period because new monuments were built, based on the Byzantine style. Often they were adorned with splendid mosaics. Today, much of this marvelous Byzantine art can still be seen in Ravenna.

Many learned men were invited to Theodoric's court to give him advice and counsel. The outstanding figure was Boethius, who came from an old noble family of Rome. Boethius had studied in Alexandria, and he was familiar with Greek philosophy and literature. In his philosophical writings he explained the logic of Aristotle to the West. In his theological writings, he used methods which would later influence western theology.

Theodoric greatly admired Boethius's talents. He often sought out Boethius for conversation at the close of his day's work. The two would spend hours talking in the porticos of the royal palace.

But the period of peace between the Ostrogoths and Romans did not last. Religion was one source of conflict. The Ostrogoths were Arians while the Romans were orthodox Catholic Christians. In Constantinople the emperor had begun to persecute Arian Christians. Another area of conflict was politics. The emperor in Constantinople feared that Theodoric might try to make Italy

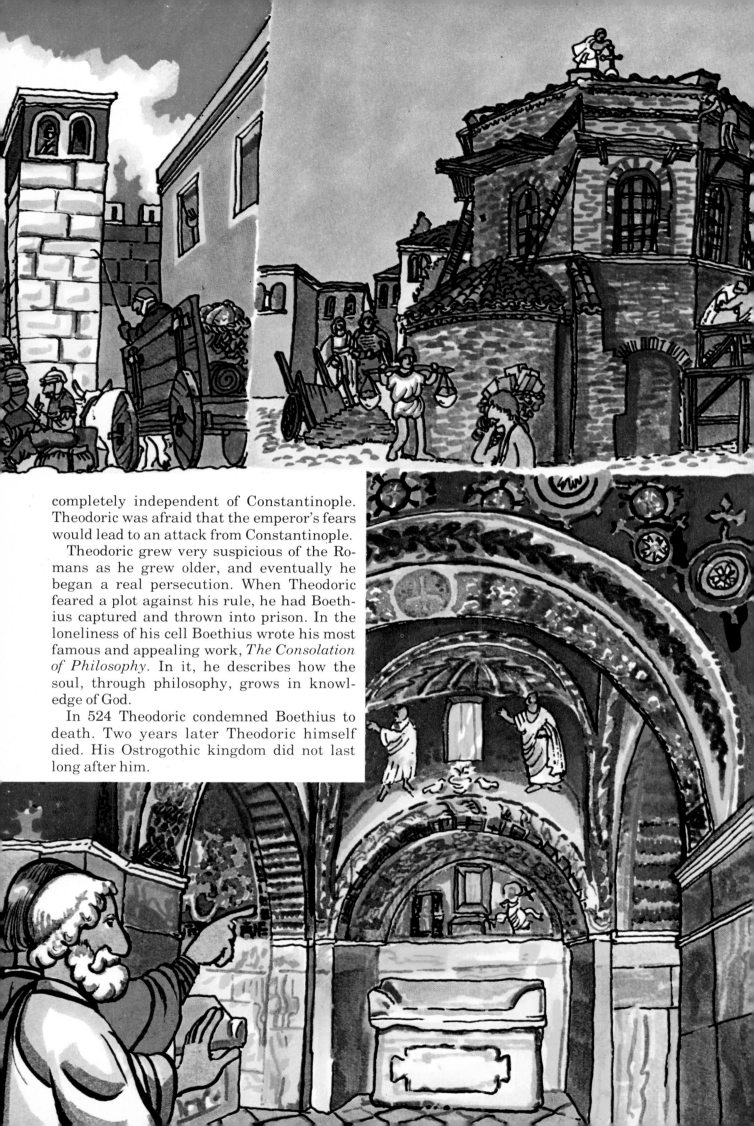

completely independent of Constantinople. Theodoric was afraid that the emperor's fears would lead to an attack from Constantinople.

Theodoric grew very suspicious of the Romans as he grew older, and eventually he began a real persecution. When Theodoric feared a plot against his rule, he had Boethius captured and thrown into prison. In the loneliness of his cell Boethius wrote his most famous and appealing work, *The Consolation of Philosophy*. In it, he describes how the soul, through philosophy, grows in knowledge of God.

In 524 Theodoric condemned Boethius to death. Two years later Theodoric himself died. His Ostrogothic kingdom did not last long after him.

32. Pope Gelasius I
led the Church
near the end
of the fifth century.
He emphasized
the difference between
the spiritual power
of the Church
and the temporal power
of the emperor.
Gelasius believed
that the bishop of Rome
had the right and duty
to guard and guide
the whole Church.

A man of strong character became pope near the end of the fifth century. Gelasius I, who was pope from 492 to 496, was a person of courage and firmness. His views continued to influence the Church for centuries after his death.

Gelasius had been secretary to two previous popes, and he supported and encouraged a firm stand in dealing with the Byzantine emperor. Writing to the emperor in the pope's name, Gelasius told the emperor that in matters of faith the emperor was to listen to the pope. A truly Christian ruler had to be obedient to the Church and its pastors in resolving religious issues.

This point of view was important in light of what was happening at the time. More and more, the emperor and his officials had tried to interfere in church matters. They sought to make the final judgment in disputes over faith and doctrine. As pope, Gelasius made it clear that the role of temporal ruler and the role of spiritual ruler were two different roles. Emperors and their civil officials had the authority to govern the empire. Bishops, especially the bishop of Rome, had the task of guiding the Church.

Gelasius stressed that the bishop of Rome had the right and duty to assume responsibility over the whole Church. The pope's responsibility was particularly clear, said Gelasius, when it came to protecting and defending Christian truths. The bishop of Rome, the successor of Peter, was the guardian of the truth which had been handed down from the apostles and explained by church councils. Gelasius said the pope had the right to correct a wayward Christian who had fallen into error. The pope had the right to decide whether a particular teaching did or did not agree with the message which Jesus Christ had given to his apostles. Gelasius's view of the papacy would leave its imprint on the Church throughout later centuries.

Gelasius I did not forget to promote good works. He sought to help the poor, to assist prisoners, and to aid strangers. He believed Jesus' word that the Christian who would be first in his kingdom should be the first to serve others. Gelasius was also a fine theologian, and is said to have written certain liturgical reforms and prayers.

33. Cassiodorus, a Roman nobleman, helped Theodoric in his work of trying to bring peace between Ostrogoths and Romans.
Later, Cassiodorus began a monastery. Its main work was to copy and preserve old manuscripts so that ancient writings would not be lost. Cassiodorus himself also wrote many books.

Flavius Magnus Aurelius Cassiodorus was born into a noble family in Calabria, southern Italy. A fine writer and scholar, he was also able and respected in political affairs. Cassiodorus knew how cruel the barbarians had been before the coming of Theodoric. He sincerely wanted to see peace between the conquered Romans and the new Ostrogothic rulers. Cassiodorus became Theodoric's minister, and he later held high offices under Theodoric's next two successors.

Toward the middle of the sixth century Cassiodorus retired from government service. He withdrew to his estates in Calabria, where he founded a monastery. Cassiodorus wanted his monastery to be a place of prayer, pious practices, and serious study. For this reason, he purchased and borrowed many manuscripts for the library which he established at his monastery. Every day his monks were to copy ancient manuscripts by hand so that the knowledge in them would not be lost.

This practice would become a major activity of monks in the West.

Cassiodorus was a practical-minded scholar with wide interests. He wanted to preserve writings of ancient culture, but he also wrote on many subjects himself. The subjects included history, law, and other liberal arts.

Cassiodorus was particularly concerned that people did not understand religious subjects. He wrote what might be called a curriculum for theological studies, as well as a summary of existing church histories. Many of his works were considered textbooks in the Middle Ages.

Cassiodorus was over ninety when he died around 580. His monastery, Vivarium, did not last long after his death. But the spirit of Cassiodorus would be carried on by many monks after him. The preservation of books and learning became the loving work of many monks in the West.

34. Benedict of Nursia
was the great organizer
of western monasticism.
With his twin sister
Scholastica, he began
the Benedictine Order.
Benedict began
to devote his life
to God as a young man,
when he went to live
a life of prayer
in a cave near Subiaco.

Benedict was one of the most important persons in the history of the western Church. The rule or way of monastic life that he began has spread throughout Europe, and his monasteries have become a source of learning, charity, and spiritual life.

Benedict and his twin sister Scholastica were born in Nursia, Italy, the children of a wealthy Roman nobleman. Scholastica devoted her life to God through prayer from the time of her childhood. Benedict was sent to Rome to study when he was about sixteen, with a companion-servant to take care of him.

This was near the close of the fifth century, and Rome was filled with pagan and Arian tribes. Many students in Rome led wild lives, and as Benedict grew older, he feared that he would take up a sinful life if he stayed there. When Benedict was about twenty, he left Rome, and with the help of his companion he found a cave in Subiaco. This place was very rocky and so extremely isolated that no one would suspect that a human being lived there. Only one person, a monk, knew where Benedict lived. This monk went to the cave daily and let down Benedict's food on a rope from a ledge above the cave.

After some years had passed, shepherds found the young hermit and talked with him, and they told others about the holy man who lived among the rocks. People began to come to Benedict for help and counsel.

Around this time, an abbot from a nearby monastery died. The monks asked Benedict to become their leader. He refused, telling them that they would not like his way of life. They would not give up, and at last he agreed to be their abbot.

As Benedict had predicted, many of the monks did not like the self-sacrificing way of life he brought to their monastery. They didn't want to give up their old way of life with enough to eat and drink, warm clothes, and a comfortable place to live. Supposedly, some of these monks tried to kill Benedict by putting poison into his wine, but Benedict blessed the wine before drinking, and the cup broke as though a stone had hit it.

This took place almost 1500 years ago, so of course we don't know exactly what happened. But it seems true that some of the monks resisted the Benedictine way of life. Benedict asked God to forgive them, and then he went back to his cave in Subiaco.

More and more people came to see him there and some settled near him, trying to live as Benedict did. Some of these people were from rich, noble families, and some were crude barbarians. Benedict realized that he had to organize a way of life for his followers, so he began to build monasteries.

35. Benedict built a large monastery on Monte Cassino. Nearby, his sister Scholastica began a convent for women. Monte Cassino was the birthplace of the Benedictine Order.

In Subiaco, Benedict built twelve monasteries for his monks, where they could live together and pray and work for the glory of God. He had heard of the eastern monks and their monasteries, and he used some of their ideas. He made some changes, according to his common sense and his experience.

One change Benedict made was to insist that his monks remain in their monasteries and not wander from place to place. Another new policy was that in addition to praying, monks in Benedict's monasteries were also responsible for working to provide their own food. At that time, people of the upper class usually did not work with their hands. Benedict ruled that all his monks must work in the fields, build, and do other manual work, whatever their social class had been. Benedict also ruled that the monks must be completely obedient to the superior or abbot. According to Benedict, the abbot had the right and duty to make final decisions.

After a few years, Benedict faced a problem from outside the monastery. A priest from a nearby church disliked Benedict because people went to the monastery church instead of to the local parish. This priest made

trouble for Benedict, and at last Benedict became afraid that his monks would be in danger.

In 529, Benedict moved to Monte Cassino, a rugged cliff in southern Italy. People in the countryside there still followed the pagan religion, but Benedict converted them to Christianity. With their help, he tore down the temple and altar to the pagan god Apollo on the top of the hill.

This was the beginning of Benedict's great new monastery, Monte Cassino. Soon other monasteries had to be built, and Benedict put his best monks in charge of them as abbots. Monte Cassino was the birthplace of the Benedictine Order, which has spread all over the world.

Benedict's twin sister, Scholastica, had always kept in touch with her brother. Now she came to southern Italy and settled in Plombariola, about five miles away from Monte Cassino. There Scholastica founded a convent for nuns. They, too, followed the Benedictine way of life. Scholastica was their leader, or abbess. Yearly, Scholastica and Benedict met in a small building between the convent and the monastery and spoke together about their orders and about spiritual things.

In Benedict's day, every monastery in the East and in the West had a rule. A rule was a set of regulations governing the way of life to be led by the monks in a particular monastery. It also offered advice and encouragement for leading a holy life.

At first the monks in Benedict's monasteries had followed his directions and had tried to imitate the example of his life. Then Benedict decided to put his Rule in writing. He wanted to maintain the changes he had introduced into his monasteries. These changes included stability, community, obedience to a superior, and manual labor. Benedict also wanted to preserve the outlook and spirit he had tried to display in his own life. A rule would help to pass this spirit along to his followers.

Benedict examined some of the most well known monastic rules then in existence. He considered those of Pachomius, Basil, and another unknown writer. After thinking about them and praying for guidance, Benedict began to set his own Rule down in writing. He dictated it to a young monk, organizing and correcting as he went along. Benedict was interested in promoting basic concepts. He wanted his monasteries to operate correctly, and he wanted to stress the importance of following Jesus. He eliminated many earlier minor regulations, so his Rule was shorter than previous ones.

Jesus was the central focus in Benedict's Rule. All the regulations and counsels were to help the monks become more and more like Jesus. Following Jesus was the central aim of monasticism, and Benedict stressed it clearly. To his monks Benedict gave two basic tasks: "Pray and work." Prayer would help his monks to love God and human beings more truly. From prayer they would receive the divine strength to love one another and other people. Work would satisfy the basic needs of daily life. It would also remove some of the temptations due to idleness.

Benedict himself probably did not intend his monks to engage in serious study and scholarship. He also would not have imagined that his monks would later become the advisers of rulers and church leaders, taking a real part in the life of the outside world. But the quality of his monks and the needs of society combined to expand the role of the Benedictines in the work of the Church and the world.

36. Benedict wrote a rule, or set of regulations, governing the way of life for his monasteries. The Benedictine Rule spread throughout the Church.

37. Many miraculous stories
are told
about Benedict's life.
Such stories may not
tell the actual facts,
but they do show
how his holiness
impressed and inspired
his followers.
Two of the stories
are told here.

Pope Gregory the Great wrote a life of Benedict. In it he included many legends told about the saint. The stories show Benedict as a man of God, a man filled with the spirit of God.

One famous legend is about Benedict and his sister Scholastica, who began a convent for women. Scholastica remained close to her brother, sharing his joys and sufferings. Once a year she asked her brother to visit her. She wanted to ask his advice and talk about spiritual things. On this particular occasion they had been together all day and it was getting late. Benedict was about to leave for his own monastery. He was getting old, and Scholastica had a feeling that this might be the last time she would see him alive. She asked him to stay, but Benedict's own Rule did not allow

a monk to remain outside his monastery overnight. Scholastica prayed that God would find some way to keep him with her longer. Suddenly a storm arose and kept Benedict from leaving. This story shows Benedict's faithfulness to his Rule, which he was unwilling to break. It also shows Scholastica's great love for Benedict and God's response to that love.

Another story concerns Benedict and two of his most faithful disciples, Placidus and Maurus. One day Placidus went to a spring to get water. He leaned too far over and fell into the water. He was in danger of drowning. From a window Benedict saw what had happened and he quickly sent Maurus to save Placidus. Maurus hurried to the spring, reached out for his friend, and brought him to shore. Only when he got back on the bank did Maurus realize that he had walked on the surface of the water. This story brings out Benedict's love for others, a love which would remain to help his followers when they needed it. The story also shows the power that comes from obeying a command with unquestioning faith. Maurus did something which seemed impossible in order to save someone in trouble.

While such stories may not be completely true, they do tell us something about the outlook and beliefs of the people who wrote them and heard them. They reveal a little about the spirit of the time in which they were popular.

38. The Byzantine Empire became stronger in every way under Emperor Justinian. One of his aims was to unite all his people in one empire and one Church, under one emperor.

In 527 Justinian became emperor in the eastern or Byzantine part of the empire. He immediately began to work toward his goal. He wanted to unite his subjects in one empire and one Church, so that all would be under the control of one emperor.

It seemed to be a good time to reform government and to restore control to a single emperor. The West had been invaded by barbarians. Internal fighting had weakened the barbarian kingdoms. But the East had a strong economy, and there was money to pay soldiers, officials, and administrators. Justinian would take advantage of these circumstances to achieve his goal of uniting the Eastern Empire.

First, Justinian needed to strengthen his own power in Constantinople and to reorganize the government. Justinian's position was uncertain at first. In 532 a riot in the hippodrome between rival groups led to a revolt. Mobs swarmed in the city. Justinian was in danger of losing the throne and his life. At this time, it seems, he lost heart. But his wife Theodora gave new courage to him and his generals. Justinian made changes to appease the mobs, and his army put down the revolt.

To reform the government, Justinian tried to stop political corruption and to appoint loyal, hard-working officials. He increased taxes so that his officials could be paid more. He tried to encourage more commerce and trade with countries to the east. And he sought to keep his eastern frontiers peaceful by paying subsidies to various countries.

As he gained control of the government, Justinian took steps to strengthen the Catholic Church. He was convinced that there should be but one Church in his empire, and that all his subjects should belong to it. He passed laws ordering pagans to prepare for Baptism and receive the sacrament. Pagan sanctuaries were transformed into Christian churches. In Athens, the famous philosophy school, which had existed since ancient, pagan times, was closed in 529. Teachers in Constantinople and elsewhere were dismissed if their views seemed unorthodox. Jews were not allowed to hold state offices, nor were others whose views were not the orthodox ones. Christians who disagreed with the Church or defended heretical views were discriminated against.

In promoting the orthodox Christian view, Justinian also tried to dominate the Church. He judged matters of faith and of church life. He proposed regulations for monastic life. He wrote sacred hymns and theological works. Justinian firmly believed in the old Byzantine tradition of imperial control over the Church. He passed this tradition on to his successors.

39. Under Justinian, Constantinople became rich and powerful— like a second Rome. Constantinople was also a center of education and culture. People from all over the empire came to Constantinople, and they were able to exchange ideas because they had the Greek language in common.

Justinian wanted to revive the glory of the Roman Empire. He and his subjects called themselves *Romaioi,* which in Greek meant "Romans." Their capital, Constantinople, was regarded as the Second Rome.

The Byzantine Empire possessed many great cities with their own cultural traditions, cities such as Alexandria, Antioch, Thessalonica, and Corinth. But by this time, many citizens thought the capital city surpassed them all. The imperial court, the patriarchal see, and the palaces of high officials provided work for artists and craftsmen. Constantinople was a center of international commerce. For centuries it would be the largest and wealthiest city in the Christian world.

The waters around the city were filled with boats. A line of fortified walls encircled the city to provide protection. Inside the city itself, the chief attraction was the imperial palace with its gardens and baths. Along the square between the palace and the city were the Church of Saint Sophia and the hippodrome. In the center of the square stood a milestone which served as the basis for measuring distances along all the roads of the empire. A large main street connected the square with the city walls, where the Golden Horn opened toward the West.

People from all over the empire came to the capital city. There were church officials visiting the patriarchal see, diplomats from the barbarian West, civil servants and leaders of the government, and nobles from the provinces visiting the emperor.

There were also many students. At the patriarchal school, students learned theology and studied sacred scripture. At the university, students learned Greek and Latin grammar, Greek philosophy, and law. The professors were famous and learned, drawing students from all over the empire.

Although Constantinople considered itself the heir of ancient Rome, its citizens spoke Greek. Almost no one used or understood Latin, even though rulers considered themselves heirs of the Roman emperors. Greek had been the language of Aristotle, Plato, and the eastern Fathers of the Church. Students from other parts of the empire who studied in Constantinople could translate works of philosophy, theology, and science from Greek into their own languages. People from different cultures shared schooling and exchanged ideas. This helped to make many people feel that they belonged to a common empire.

40. One of Justinian's
greatest achievements
was his reform
of Roman law.
Justinian had scholars
gather and study
all Roman laws, and
then combine them
into one collection.
We call this collection
The Code of Justinian.
It was the basis
of law in Byzantium
for almost 1000 years,
and was important
in western law, too.

One of Justinian's most important and longest-lasting achievements was the creation of the *Corpus Juris Civilis,* or *Body of Civil Law*. This was a collection of imperial laws and legal opinions that replaced existing law codes in the empire. Justinian wanted to have one body of law that could be followed throughout his territories.

The work of gathering and writing the *Corpus Juris Civilis* was tremendous. A team of jurists, or experts on the law, worked on it for five years. They gathered the documents and records on the law and read them all—perhaps as many as 2000 documents.

The jurists took out laws that were no longer usable or sensible, combined laws that belonged together, and compiled everything into one code, divided into three parts.

The first part contained all the imperial edicts or laws put out by the emperors from Hadrian to Justinian that were still in force.

The second part contained the best legal opinions of Roman lawyers on cases that had been tried before courts. These opinions were just as good as laws and would be used to settle similar cases.

The third part was a textbook of legal principles to be studied by those who wished to become lawyers and work for the government.

This great legal work was based on records and laws of the past, but Justinian put some of his own ideas in it. He included the idea that the emperor had absolute power, an idea unknown to Roman law. And the influence of Christian ideas could be seen in the laws.

The *Corpus Juris Civilis,* which is now called *The Code of Justinian,* was the governing law of Byzantium for 1000 years. And beginning around the year 1100, Justinian's code of law gradually became the basis of law for the countries of the western world.

41. Justinian sent armies to take back lands that had been conquered by barbarian Ostrogoths, Vandals, and Visigoths. Under Justinian's reign, the countries around the Mediterranean Sea were united under one ruler.

Justinian worked in the Eastern Empire to increase the power of the emperor, reform the government, and strengthen the Church. He also raised armies in order to reconquer imperial lands that had been taken by the barbarians. Before setting this plan in motion, Justinian made peace with the empire's long-standing enemy to the East, Persia, the country now called Iran. Then a large army and navy were carefully organized under the leadership of two outstanding generals, Belisarius and Narses. As an excuse for launching an attack, Justinian would side with some member of a ruling family who was fighting another family member for the throne in a given country.

Justinian's reconquest of the West began with an attack on the kingdom of the Vandals in North Africa. It was successful, and

Justinian's forces moved on to Italy, which was governed by the Ostrogoths. After many battles, Justinian's armies won a decisive victory over the Ostrogoths in Umbria.

Around the same time, other Byzantine armies were successfully fighting the Visigoths in Spain. They managed to regain the islands and the most important ports of southeastern Spain.

By this time it seemed that Justinian's dream of a united empire would come true once and for all. Politically and culturally the Byzantine Empire was the dominant power in the Mediterranean world. Imperial attempts to regain the West had been successful. Some Germanic kingdoms had disappeared; others had suffered setbacks. Gaul still lay beyond imperial control, but the Merovingians — the ruling family in Gaul — did not cause trouble for the empire.

But the reunification of the empire had cost vast amounts money and many human lives. The empire was deeply in debt, and its subjects were worn out and discontented. Soon the Western Empire would be lost again. The Berbers in North Africa were in revolt against the Byzantines, and within a century North Africa would be conquered by Arab Muslims. In Spain the Visigoths were moving out from the interior to recapture the coastal areas of the southeast. The defeat of the Ostrogoths in Italy allowed the peninsula to be invaded by other barbarian tribes. In 568 the Lombards would enter as conquerors. In the Balkans the Byzantine forces were too few to withstand later invasions by the Avars and the Slavs.

TOLEDO

RAVENNA

CONSTANTINOPLE

ROMAN EMPIRE
VISIGOTHIC KINGDOMS
FRANKISH KINGDOMS
LOMBARDS

42. Christian art and architecture flourished in the Byzantine Empire under Justinian's rule. Many basilicas were built. The most famous is Saint Sophia, built in Constantinople.

The grandeur of Justinian's imperial rule found its best expression in the arts—in the use of space and in vivid decoration and color. Byzantine artists created splendid visions of a world made glorious by the presence of God.

Architects produced the most important art works and the most interesting innovations of this period. Hundreds of churches

Some churches had four square sides, others had five sides, some were even built in the form of a cross. During this period architects in Constantinople and the East successfully solved the problem of placing one or more domes on top of the church buildings. Basilicas and other church buildings arose everywhere in the empire, but the most beautiful ones were to be found in Ravenna, Constantinople, and Salonica.

A most striking and famous example of the new imperial architecture was built in Constantinople. At the request of Justinian, two architects— Anthemius of Tralles and Isidorus of Miletus—rebuilt the cathedral of Saint Sophia. The Greek name *Sophia* means "Holy Wisdom of God." This magnificent church, topped by an enormous dome thirty-one meters (about thirty-four yards) in diameter, was consecrated on December 27, 537. The church building of Saint Sophia still exists as a museum in Istanbul, the name by which Constantinople is called today.

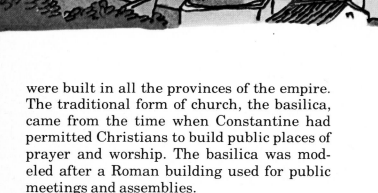

were built in all the provinces of the empire. The traditional form of church, the basilica, came from the time when Constantine had permitted Christians to build public places of prayer and worship. The basilica was modeled after a Roman building used for public meetings and assemblies.

The basilica was a very long rectangular building divided into three or more aisles by rows of columns. Often there were galleries reserved for women on either side above the aisles. The central aisle, or nave, was the widest and highest. A series of windows above it permitted light to flow into the interior. The entrance was at one end. At the other end was the apse, where the Eucharist was celebrated. The apse in a basilica was usually shaped like a half-circle. In the center of the apse was the bishop's chair. The altar was a plain table placed between the apse and the nave.

43.
Byzantine art during the reign of Justinian took many forms, such as carved ivory, wall paintings called frescoes, painted pictures or icons, mosaics made of many small pieces of glass, and beautiful golden jewelry. Much of the art was religious.

Art in the time of Emperor Justinian took many forms besides church buildings. Artists borrowed elements of the classical Greek and Roman tradition, but the final result was a mixture of classical techniques, Christian themes, and new forms. Sculpture of a completely Roman type was looked upon with suspicion because it seemed to preserve traces of paganism.

Many ivory reliefs were created. These were small or large works, often depicting scenes from history or the Bible. One famous example was the ivory work on the throne of the archbishop of Ravenna. Other typical art works of the period were the miniature pictures in manuscripts, icons, frescoes, and wall mosaics.

Icons were pictures on wooden tablets. Often the colors used in them were mixed with wax to make them shine. The pictures were of Jesus or of some holy person such as Mary, or of a saint. Few icons from this period have survived to our own day. Most of the ones we have from this period come to us from Egypt and the monasteries around Mount Sinai. At first most icons showed only a portrait of the person. Gradually the artists grew more concerned with bringing out the spiritual ideas in their work. They tried to represent some biblical event in the icon, or show a biblical person who could be recognized by the things in the picture. They began to put initials or symbols alongside a figure, so that it would be immediately recognized. Or else they might use specific colors that people would associate with a certain holy person. Icons thus allowed people to ponder their faith as they gazed on the pictures.

Frescoes were paintings on wet plaster made with lime. As the plaster dried, the paint combined with the lime in the plaster.

Much more costly were mosaics. They were vivid and striking works. Small pieces of multi-colored glass were combined to form a beautiful design. Light glinting in the finished work hinted at the splendor of the divine world. In Justinian's time, mosaics were used to decorate the walls of churches as well as the apses. Shining mosaics of saints, emperors, Jesus, and Mary adorned the newly built basilicas. Mosaic art flourished in Ravenna as well as in Constantinople. For there the power and glory of the revived empire was supposed to shine as clearly as in the great eastern city. Ravenna was also a center from which Byzantine forms of art spread to other parts of Italy and the West.

Goldsmiths produced many beautiful works of jewelry and decorated materials. Enameled works, decorated fabrics, inlaid and chiseled products were also produced. The techniques and lessons of the ancient classical world were being used to create the art forms of the Christian empire.

44. The Byzantine rulers tried to control religion. The emperor in Constantinople felt that he had the right to decide how all his people should believe and act. But different religious views developed in some countries such as Egypt, Persia, Syria, and Armenia.

In the West, the basic Roman approach to life seemed to be a practical one. People were concerned with concrete, daily life and with organization. Once they became Christians, people in the West did not get involved in many arguments about the basic truths of the Christian faith. The arrival of Arian barbarians raised problems, but eventually the barbarians were converted to the Catholic version of Christianity.

The situation was different in the East, including Egypt. The East had been the birthplace of Christianity. It was also the home of several cultural centers. Even after the Roman conquest these peoples con-

tinued to ponder and debate questions of culture and religion. They were anxious to preserve their own way of life and view of things. The emperors in Constantinople wanted to impose their views on all in order to avoid riots and revolts. But bishops, monks, and ordinary Christians in different cultural areas were just as anxious to preserve their own views.

Various religious ideas developed in Egypt, Syria, Armenia, and Persia. Sometimes these ideas were very different from the views held as correct by the Church as a whole and expressed by church councils. The local eastern churches were alive and active, and they did not hesitate to stick firmly to their views and try to spread them to others.

One view, known as Monophysitism, had great influence in Syria, for example. It was condemned by the Council of Chalcedon because it held that Jesus was truly God but not truly a human being. Around 650, Bishop Jacob (or James) Baradai of Alexandria spread his own version of Monophysitism in Egypt. He was supported by Theodora, wife of Emperor Justinian. Jacob formed a Church that has been known since that time as the Jacobite Church.

45. An Armenian Church
arose in Asia Minor
and a Coptic Church
grew in Egypt. In Persia,
believers in the Nestorian
heresy began a Church.
In these countries,
we can still see
pieces of religious art
made long ago,
when these Churches
first began.

The Monophysite heresy was quite successful in Egypt. It was popular in the city of Alexandria and the surrounding area. Alexandria had been a major center of Christianity, but gradually Constantinople became more important as the political and religious capital of the East. Church leaders and people of Alexandria certainly did not like having to take second place.

In the sixth century a Coptic Church arose in Egypt, taking its name from the word *coptic,* meaning native Egyptian. It was separate from the Catholic Church. Justinian opposed it, but the monks and people of Egypt worked together to fashion and strengthen their own Church. Though Muslim invaders would later persecute both Catholic and Coptic Christians, the Coptic Church has survived for more than a thousand years. In recent centuries, one part of the Coptic Church rejoined the Catholic Church. Today the Catholic Copts have their own church organization under the pope's leadership, but they follow the rites and practices of the Coptic Church.

The Armenian Church has its own distinctive and interesting history. Its traditions remain alive among the people who live in the rugged area in Asia Minor between the Anatolian plateau and the Iranian plateau. Some Christians may have arrived there in the first part of the second century, but the conversion of the Armenian people to Christianity really took place during the third century. It was largely due to a native Armenian, Gregory, who is nicknamed The Illuminator. He himself was a convert and he managed finally to convert the Armenian king, Tiridates. The king quickly turned Christianity into the official religion of his country and aided Gregory in his work of converting the population. Eventually the Armenian Church adopted its own version of Monophysitism. Its patriarch, residing in the city of Dvin, became the supreme religious authority and was known as the *katholikos*.

A separate national Church also arose in Persia, which is now Iran. Around the turn of the sixth century some Christian followers of the Nestorian heresy fled to Persia. Nestorians believed that Jesus was two separate persons, one divine and one human. The Catholic Church had decided that this was a heresy, but the Nestorians established a church in Nineveh and spread its teaching into India and Ceylon.

46. In spite of divisions
within the Church,
the Byzantines were
deeply religious.
Their spirituality
was expressed
in liturgical prayers
and hymns,
in their veneration
for the sacred mysteries
and the saints,
and in other forms
of devotion.

During the fifth and sixth centuries the Byzantine liturgy acquired the features that make it so very distinctive and appealing. A number of beautiful hymns were written, including one that may have been composed by the Emperor Justinian himself. It centers on the idea of Jesus as the only begotten Son of God and shows how very much the people believed in Jesus.

Another beautiful hymn written at this time is the *Hymn of the Cherubim,* which is sung in preparation for Communion. Humility was a characteristic of Byzantine life, and it is captured in such prayers as this one:

Accept me today, O Son of God,
   as a sharer in your mystical supper.
For I will not speak of your mystery
   to your enemies,
Nor will I give you a kiss,
   as did Judas.
Rather, like the thief I will say to you:
   Remember me, O Lord, in your kingdom.

A ceremony still used in the Catholic Church today on Good Friday, the unveiling of the cross and veneration of it, began in the Byzantine Church. For many centuries, some of the prayers at this ceremony were sung in Greek in the Roman Catholic Church.

The practice of having processions in church during Mass comes from Byzantine ceremonies in the fifth and sixth centuries.

Another part of Byzantine devotion was the use of sacred images in paying reverence to God and the saints. The early Christians did not use images in their religious worship for fear of confusion or idolatry. But by the sixth century sacred images were being used in many places as a way of expressing devotion to God and sacred realities. People in the Byzantine Church used icons or painted religious pictures to pray worshipfully to God and the saints.

The religious life of the people was also expressed in their liking for lives of the saints. Many of these stories were highly fictional and legendary. Church authorities often had reservations about them, but the people loved the stories anyway.

Thus the religious devotion of the people at this time was just as real as the arguments and the divisions in the Church were. In general, it would seem that the people wanted something visible, something they could touch that would help them live their religion. In concrete ways, they tried to make their beliefs part of everyday life.

47.
Emperor Justinian began
a series of wars
to win back territory
taken over by barbarians.
He reconquered several
countries, and he made
Catholic Christianity
free and strong again
in those lands.
But Justinian treated
other religions harshly.

The Vandals of North Africa had continued to persecute the Christian Church and its leaders. Emperor Justinian felt that the Vandals had become weaker than they once were. One of his first military moves in the West was to send troops under his general, Belisarius, against the Vandals. Belisarius defeated the Vandals.

It became possible once again for Catholic Christianity to flourish in North Africa. Bishops and priests living in exile returned to guide their fellow Christians and to win back those who had been forcibly converted to Arianism. Goods and property were restored to the North African Church. Arian priests and bishops who agreed to give up Arian beliefs were allowed to become members of the Catholic Church. They had to be lay people now, but the Church assumed the responsibility of supporting them.

Heretics and non-Christians were not treated so well. Their places of worship were closed down, and cultural or educational activities were forbidden. Justinian did not look with favor on Jews, pagans, Arians, or Donatists, and he treated them harshly.

Once Belisarius returned to Constantinople, many revolts broke out in North Africa. Arian and Donatist clergymen sometimes encouraged or even led such revolts. Even the Catholic bishops did not have a united viewpoint or approach, and disagreements with the emperor arose. Justinian formulated his own theological views, demanded acceptance of them, and exiled bishops who would not go along with him. Justin, the next emperor, continued the same basic policy. He and his imperial officials sought to keep tight control over the Church.

48. The Arian Visigothic
king in Spain
tried to unite
his kingdom by forcing
all his people to become
Arians. The king even
had his own son killed
when the prince
became a Catholic.
Arians and Catholic
Christians continued
to be in conflict.

The Byzantine Empire had conquered the southern coast of the Iberian or Spanish peninsula, and some islands off the coast in the Mediterranean Sea. Byzantium was not able to conquer the interior of Spain, where two barbarian kingdoms existed. One was the kingdom of the Suevi, the other was the kingdom of the Visigoths.

The Suevi had a small kingdom in the northwest part of the Iberian peninsula. Part of their kingdom is today northern Portugal. The Suevi were Arian Christians, but Catholic Christians were allowed to live freely in their territory. In 550, the Suevi king became a Catholic Christian, and a little while later a monk named Martin came to live among the Suevi and spread Catholic Christianity.

The kingdom of the Visigoths was larger. It included much of the Iberian peninsula and extended northward into present-day France. The Visigoths were Arians, and there was great tension between them and the native Catholic people. At first, the Visigoths kept themselves separate from the natives, and marriage between Visigoths and Catholics

was forbidden. The Visigoths had their own laws and customs, and the local people lived according to Roman law and followed their customs. As time went on, the Visigoths began to marry Catholic natives, in spite of the law. Some Visigoths became Catholics, and some even became church officials.

In 568, Leovigild, a strong leader, became king of the Visigoths. He conquered the Suevi and took back some land from the Byzantines. Leovigild wanted to unify his kingdom under one set of laws and one religion — and the religion was to be Arian Christianity.

Catholic Christianity continued to win converts. One convert was Leovigild's eldest son, Hermenegild, who was ruler of part of the Visigothic kingdom. Hermenegild married Igunda, a Frankish princess who was a Catholic. Within a short time, Hermenegild also became a Catholic, greatly angering his father. War began, and King Leovigild won. Hermenegild was taken prisoner. He refused to give up his new faith, so his father had him killed on Easter Sunday in 585.

49. At this time,
the number of parishes
increased greatly,
and the eucharistic
liturgy and other
sacred services were
offered more regularly.
For the first time
priests as well as bishops
were allowed to preach.

Even before 300, in some of the larger cities of the Roman Empire such as Rome, Carthage, Alexandria, and Antioch, there began to be the type of local church that we now know as a parish. But the real development of parish life in urban and rural areas came during the fourth, fifth, and sixth centuries. It was then that priests and deacons began to provide a variety of functions and services for people in local communities. They took over pastoral and liturgical duties that had once belonged only to bishops.

The situation varied from place to place, of course. But priests began to offer the

eucharistic liturgy and other sacred services more regularly. Christians were expected to attend church on a more regular basis for these services, which included various prayer services in which the psalms were used.

Priests now were authorized to preach, a duty which once had been reserved for bishops alone. Priests were also expected to help train future priests and deacons, and simple parish schools were begun for this purpose.

The growth of parishes enabled Christians to live in closer union with each other and to share the expression of their faith. It was easier for them to receive the sacraments and join in prayer. The parish provided them with a place of refuge and support, a place to get material and spiritual help. In particular, parishes in rural areas helped Christians to feel less cut off from the life of the Christian community in more developed areas.

50. Under King Clovis and his successors, the Church grew steadily in Gaul, but there was little direct contact with the pope. The Church in Gaul worked closely with the government, and many bishops and priests came from noble families.

Under Clovis and his successors, the Church grew steadily in Gaul. Clovis and the family of rulers who followed him in Frankish Gaul were called Merovingians. The name came from the grandfather of Clovis, whose name was Merwig.

During the first years of Merovingian rule, priests and bishops in Frankish Gaul had to come from other regions, where the Church had existed longer and was stronger. As years passed, the Church in Gaul became able to provide its own priests.

At this time in Gaul, most of the priests and practically all of the bishops came from noble or wealthy families. One reason for this was that a priest had to have some education. He had to be able to read and write, at the least. Wealthy families could usually provide education for their children, and so the vocation of priesthood seemed more natural among them.

Nevertheless, parish priests could and did come from the common people. The son of a farmer, a shipbuilder, or any laborer could become a priest if he fulfilled certain conditions. These conditions were: he had to want to serve God as a priest; he had to be of good character, or at least resolve to put aside any bad practices of his past; the bishop had to accept him as a priest-to-be; and the king had to give his permission.

For a long time, most of the bishops in Gaul came from the noble families. Some of the bishops were extremely wealthy in their own right. Such a bishop, if he wished, might use his wealth to build churches in his diocese.

It was around this time that clergymen—men such as deacons and priests, who had taken Holy Orders—began to dress in a way that marked them off from lay people. Also, if a clergyman was taken to court, he was not judged by the law of the land or region, but he was tried according to Roman law.

An ordained priest was sent to a specific church by his bishop, and he was not supposed to leave it without written permission from his bishop. Priests were not allowed to wander from place to place as they wished. If they did so, they faced being punished by the local and national church councils.

In Merovingian Gaul, the Church was really a local church, and its leaders were carefully watched by the king. The Church recognized and honored the pope as the chief bishop, but the pope had little direct dealing with Christians in Gaul. Until the time of Pope Gregory the Great, Arles was the only diocese in Gaul that was closely connected with the pope. The other Frankish bishops ran their diocesan churches in fairly independent ways.

**51. Bishops in Gaul were
very important persons.
Besides ruling
the local church,
they often had much to say
about town government.
Sometimes they served
as judges and some even
directed public works.**

The bishop was the chief of the clergy in a local area in Gaul. His diocese was usually centered around an old Roman town or camp. As Christianity spread, new bishops and dioceses were created.

Bishops were supposed to be elected by the clergy and the people of the area. In reality, the kings made their wishes clear to the electors and often appointed their own favorite candidates directly. Sometimes they selected the best man for the job, but sometimes they were bribed. Gregory of Tours tells us that the office of bishop was often sold by the king to the person who was willing to pay most for it. Local and national church councils tried to stop this. The compromise solution was that the king had the right to approve or disapprove the candidate who had been properly elected.

Many bishops were worthy of their impor-

tant office. The bishop had tight control over his clergy. He really governed the Church in his diocese, with the help of his priests and special assistants. He had charge of church goods and property, which often were worth a great deal. Kings, nobles, and landlords made generous contributions to the Church. Once property had been given to the Church, it could not be taken back. At first all such donations belonged primarily to the bishop and his diocese. Gradually local donations to a parish church or chapel were regarded as belonging to that particular local church. Ordinary people, too, often gave gifts to the church, donating such things as bread, cheese, wool, or animals.

In his episcopal see, which was usually a town, a bishop performed important civic functions as well. He provided education at parish schools, taught by parish priests. He acted as a town administrator and took care of such public works as existed. The bishop often served as a judge of local disputes. People trusted his fairness more than they trusted that of the local count, who should have been the judge. The bishop could also give refuge in his church to those accused of crimes. This right of sanctuary was respected because people feared that God would punish them severely if they violated a church.

More important, perhaps, was the fact that the bishop and his priests offered help to various groups which needed protectors. These included widows, orphans, the poor, slaves, and captives. Often the poor were gathered into an organized body, and their names were registered on a special church list. Thus the diocese and its bishop performed useful and necessary social work which otherwise might have been totally neglected.

52. Pilgrimages to shrines of saints began to become more widespread in the Church at this time, and Christian Franks took part in this devotion. Also, the number of Frankish monasteries grew rapidly. Usually each monastery was independent of others and was under the rule of the local bishop.

Going on a pilgrimage, an act of religious devotion, was becoming more widespread in the Church at this time. A pilgrimage was a trip—often on foot—to a holy place, usually the place where a saint had lived and died. The pilgrim went to give thanks to God, to ask for a special blessing, or sometimes to do penance for sin. Sometimes an interested priest or bishop would preach about pilgrimage to a parish, urging all members to go on the pilgrimage in a group, praying and singing together on their way.

One of the first recorded Christian pilgrimages is that of Queen Helena, mother of Constantine the Great. She went to Palestine and Judea in 326, to visit the places where Jesus had lived. In Rome, the sites venerated as the graves of Peter and Paul were also places of pilgrimage. In times to come, people would travel from as far away as Britain to visit the graves of these two great apostles.

At this time in Gaul, the tomb of Martin of Tours was sometimes a place of pilgrimage for the Franks. Martin had been a monk who became bishop of Tours near the end of the fourth century. As bishop, he encouraged the spread of monasticism in the country around Tours.

After Clovis became a Catholic Christian around 496, the number of monasteries in Gaul increased. New monastic houses for men and women were founded by kings, bishops, and private persons who could afford the expense.

Each of these monasteries was under the final authority of the local bishop. The first head of the monastery—called "abbot" for men, and "abbess" for women—was often chosen by the person or church official who founded the monastery and contributed to its support. As the years passed, the new abbots and abbesses would be chosen by the family of the founder, or by the person who held that church office. Sometimes the monastic community elected its own head person, but the election had to be approved by the bishop in charge of the monastery.

These early monasteries in Gaul were independent of one another. Each had its own rule, based upon the earlier ones of Pachomius, Basil, Cassian, and Caesar of Arles. The monasteries offered a quiet life of prayer and mediation for those who wished to withdraw from the world. These monasteries did not try to spread their influence to society at large in any active, direct way.

Greater organization and federation of monasteries would come around 585, with the arrival of the Irish monk, Columbanus. He built or reformed many monasteries around Gaul, promoting more missionary activity in the world at the same time. The Rule of St. Benedict did not become a part of monastic life in Gaul until the seventh century. Eventually Louis, the son of Charlemagne, would bring the Benedictine Rule to all monasteries in his kingdom. Then French monastic life would be ready for its great flowering during the Middle Ages.

53. Parish life of Frankish
    Christians was active
    and varied.
    They were enthusiastic
    in attending Mass,
    church services, and
    sacramental rites.
    They believed in prayer
    and they had great respect
    for their bishop.

Frankish Christians were enthusiastic followers of their religion. They believed in prayer and devotion to the saints. They had great respect for church leaders, holy things, and relics. The growing parish life in Gaul was active and varied, and some changes were taking place in the use of the sacraments.

Baptism, which once had taken place only in the cathedral church (the bishop's church), was now part of local parish life. Infants and young children were now baptized as a matter of course. Easter was the main time for Baptism, but Baptisms also took place at Christmas and on the feasts of various saints.

Often parents would prepare for a child's Baptism for a week or more, fasting and taking part in the liturgy daily.

The Anointing of the Sick was also practiced. Holy oil, which had been blessed on the feast of Saints Cosmas and Damian, both of whom had been doctors, was rubbed on the body of a sick person to heal illness and ward off demons. This ceremony may also have been intended to lead the faithful away from pagan forms of magic.

Frankish Christians were urged to prepare carefully for receiving Communion. They were encouraged to receive the Eucharist on the feasts of martyrs and other great saints.

54. Our history of the rise
of the Islamic religion
and the Muslim empire
begins with a description
of Arab life and religion.

The Arabian peninsula lay in southwest Asia between the Red Sea and the Indian Ocean. Its main physical feature, then as now, was a large desert plateau bordered by steep mountainous areas on the south and west. Rainfall was scarce, and the meager streams were supplied with water only in the rainy season.

The harsh interior had been occupied for centuries by various tribes who wandered from place to place. These tribes lived a hard and rugged life as they sought out water and food for their herds. They had a deep liking for adventure and heroic deeds. They admired independence and courage. And they sometimes raided the camps or villages of more settled peoples.

Arab peoples were organized into tribes, clans, and extended families. All the members of a given clan were under the authority of an elder, who governed with the aid of a council. Herds and wells belonged to a tribe or a whole clan rather than to one individual. Each tribe maintained relations with other tribes, arranged marriages, and insured justice for its members.

The Arabs also engaged in trade. Their peninsula was located along the routes that connected the Far East, Africa, and the Mediterranean. Some Arabs had settled down in the rich commercial centers and towns that had grown up. One of the chief cities was Mecca.

In religion these desert peoples have been called *polytheists,* from two Greek words meaning "many gods," because they seemed to worship more than one god. Their religious worship varied from place to place. They worshiped local gods and goddesses and revered places and objects which were felt to contain divine power. They also made pilgrimages to places where they believed the divine power showed forth in a special way.

This is a very brief summary of some of the religious ideas among the Arabs before the seventh century. Like the religious life of many nations, it was far more complex in reality.

55. Christianity entered the Arab world from Ethiopia and Syria. While the examples of religious hermits and monks appealed to the Arabs, Christianity did not become their unifying religion.

The Arab tribes had gradually learned about Christianity. When the Ethiopians invaded Yemen in the sixth century, they brought Christianity with them. They also built a church, which became a center of pilgrimage for Arab Christians. This competed with the traditional places of Arab pilgrimage, and particularly with the popular pagan temple at Mecca.

Christianity's major influence in Arabia came from Byzantine territory to the north. From 500 on, there was an important trade route from Damascus, Syria, to southern Arabia called the Incense Road. Syrian and Arabian merchants met at commercial centers along this route.

In the border area between Byzantine territory and the Persian Empire some semi-nomadic Arab tribes had converted to Christianity in its Monophysite form. Farther east, another group of Nestorian Christians sent missionaries to India and the Arab peninsula. Scattered Christian communities formed there.

But perhaps the most important Christian influence was that of Syrian monks. The simple, austere life of religious hermits and ascetics was somewhat like that of the Bedouins in the desert. Religious exercises such as fasting, genuflecting, and reciting short prayers and litanies also appealed to the desert dwellers. Some Arabs who converted to Christianity became monks. After 500 there may even have been an Arab bishop who followed the tribes in their wanderings.

But Christianity did not win over the vast majority of Arabs. They remained loyal, for the most part, to their various local religious practices and traditions.

56. Around the year 610,
    Mohammed began to preach
    the religion of Islam,
    or submission to God,
    among the Arabs.
    The city of Medina
    became Mohammed's
    headquarters, and Arabs
    in great numbers joined
    the new religion.

The disorganized situation of the Arab tribes changed greatly in the seventh century because of the message and work of an Arab named Mohammed (or Muhammad). His story is placed here, at the end of the sixth century, because the work of Mohammed contributed greatly to the final disappearance of the ancient Greek and Roman world in the Mediterranean.

Mohammed was a wealthy Arabian who lived in Mecca, a city with an important Arab shrine or holy place. Mohammed did much traveling, made many contacts with Arab tribes, and encountered their differing beliefs. He also gained some knowledge of Judaism, and learned about the Monophysite version of Christianity.

Around the age of forty Mohammed had visionary experiences which convinced him that he had been selected by God to be the prophet of the true religion for the Arab peoples. The revelations told Mohammed

that there was only one God, who was "the God" (*al-ilah* in Arabic). It was wrong to worship many gods. One must surrender in total "submission" (*islam* in Arabic) to Allah, who is good and merciful and who will reward the good and punish the wicked.

At first Mohammed felt very close to Jews and Christians, but they did not welcome his message and adopt it. Many Arabs opposed Mohammed and his life was in danger so long as he lived in Mecca. Some people in the city of Yathrib were more open to his message. When a severe quarrel between different tribes broke out there, the citizens of Yathrib asked Mohammed to settle the dispute. They vowed to accept his decision and also agreed to protect him and his small band of loyal followers as if they were members of their own families.

When Mohammed arrived in 622, the city was renamed the City of the Prophet (*Madinat-an-Nabi* in Arabic), or Medina. Mohammed's departure from Mecca for Yathrib is called the *hejira*.

In the city of Medina the religion of Islam began to grow. Mohammed proclaimed the divine messages he heard from Allah, and he also began to set down guidelines for social and political life. More and more Arabs joined his cause, though he had some defeats, and the city of Mecca opposed him.

In 629, Mohammed went to Mecca and won more followers there. The next year, he marched victoriously into Mecca with his followers and took over as its Arab leader. Until his death in 632, Mohammed continued to proclaim his message. Arab converts flocked to the true worship of Allah: Islam.

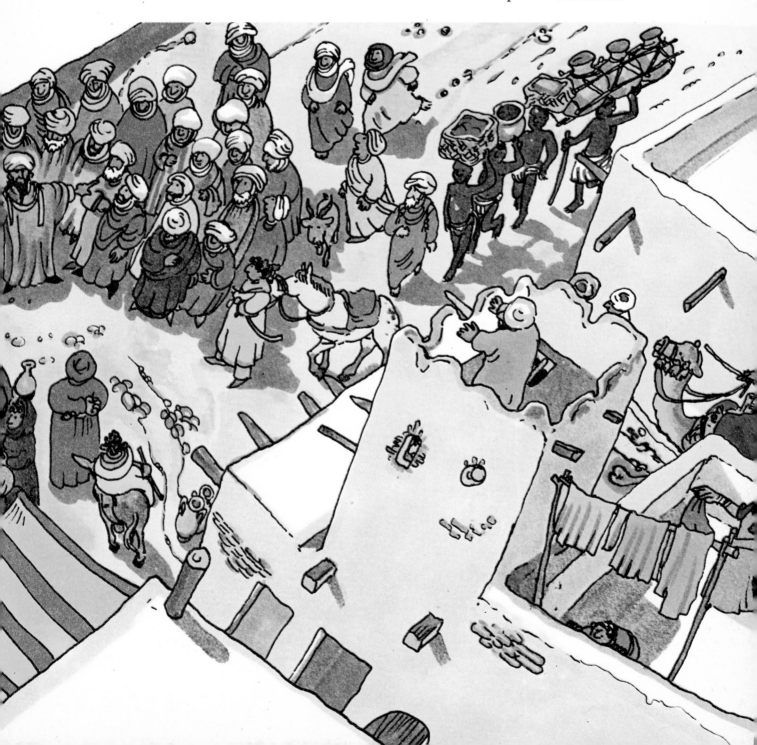

57. After Mohammed's death, his preaching was written in a book called the Koran. The Muslims also collected the sayings of Mohammed into a book, and wrote the story of his life.

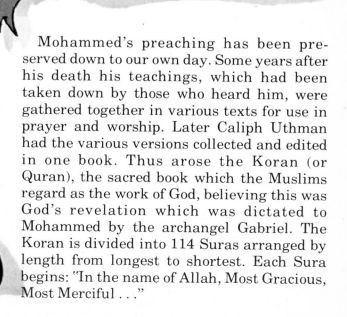

Mohammed's preaching has been preserved down to our own day. Some years after his death his teachings, which had been taken down by those who heard him, were gathered together in various texts for use in prayer and worship. Later Caliph Uthman had the various versions collected and edited in one book. Thus arose the Koran (or Quran), the sacred book which the Muslims regard as the work of God, believing this was God's revelation which was dictated to Mohammed by the archangel Gabriel. The Koran is divided into 114 Suras arranged by length from longest to shortest. Each Sura begins: "In the name of Allah, Most Gracious, Most Merciful . . ."

The Muslims also compiled a life of Mohammed and a collection of his sayings. This collection is the foundation for the body of Islamic tradition known as the *Sunna*.

Mohammed's teaching contained several basic ideas that Islam still teaches. First of all, Mohammed was a prophet, the last in a long line of prophets stretching from Abraham to Jesus. He preached that there is only one God, who is completely beyond the reach of human beings but close to their hearts. He opposed the Christian view of God as the Trinity. Jesus, he believed, was miraculously born of the Virgin Mary but not truly divine.

In their daily lives Muslims were to follow the five basic duties of Islam. First came the profession of faith: "There is no God but Allah, and Mohammed is His Prophet." Then there was daily prayer at fixed hours of the day, involving certain bodily postures. Third, Muslims should make a pilgrimage to Mecca at least once during their lifetime, if possible. Fourth, Muslims should fast during the month of Ramadan, the ninth month of the Muslim year; it should be a total fast from sunrise to sunset. Fifth, Muslims should give alms for pious and charitable purposes. These were the duties of the Muslim community of believers.

58. The Muslim Arabs spread
their religion
and their rule
north, east, and west,
conquering Persian and
Byzantine lands.
The territories
reconquered by Justinian
were now lost forever
to the Eastern Empire.
The city of Damascus
became the capital
of the Arab Muslims.

Mohammed had succeeded in welding together many different and sometimes opposing tribes into a single religious people. Its members were Muslims, followers of Islam, a religion based on giving total submission to Allah.

The Muslim community soon felt a need to expand their numbers and boundaries after the death of Mohammed. He had handed on his spiritual and political leadership to his

successors, who had intense religious zeal. They devoted all their energy to spreading the Islamic doctrine. The Muslim religion was to be transmitted to others, no matter what the cost in energy. A war to spread the faith was regarded as necessary and worthy.

After the death of Mohammed, a series of ongoing wars and victories gave the Arab Muslims control over surrounding empires. In an amazingly short time, their rule extended far beyond their homeland.

The first successors of Mohammed were Abu Bakr and Omar. Omar was a man of great religious zeal, and he in particular promoted Arab expansion in the Middle East. His brave general, Khalid al Walid, led an Arab army into Syria, which was then a rich Byzantine province. In 635 the Arab army won the bloody battle of Yarmuk in Syria and entered the city of Damascus in triumph. The Byzantine Empire had lost Syria forever.

With the same dash and speed Arab armies conquered Iraq, Persia, Egypt, and the area of present-day Lybia. Then the Arab armies turned westward and swept along the coast of North Africa to the Atlantic Ocean. The lands which Justinian's armies had regained in the sixth century were lost to Byzantium in little more than a hundred years.

In a relatively short space of time the Muslims had created a huge empire. They moved their capital to Damascus in Syria.

59. The Arabian conquest and the spread of Islam marked the close of the Greek-Roman world and the dream of a single Christian empire in the region around the Mediterranean. Islam, Judaism, and Christianity were now the religions of the countries in that area, and there would be continuing conflict among them.

The conquests achieved by the followers of Islam had great consequences for the Mediterranean world. The dream of such emperors as Theodosius and Justinian would not be fulfilled. The Christian peoples living around the Mediterranean Sea would not be united in one political empire under one Christian ruler. Now many Christians and former Christians found themselves under Muslim rule. The lands of Islam now included some of the oldest Christian communities: Antioch, Edessa, Alexandria, and Jerusalem. Moreover, the military presence of Muslims in the Mediterranean made contacts between the West and Byzantium more difficult. The two areas of Christendom grew further apart, and this may have helped widen the division between the Eastern Church and the Western Church.

But the appearance of Islam changed the basic framework of the ancient Greek and Roman world. Now three major religions dominated the scene: Islam, Judaism, and Christianity. Though there were differences between these religions, they shared several significant features.

First of all, each religion had a sacred book which was regarded as the word of God. In it God had revealed what people should believe and do. The Jews had the Old Testament. Christians had the Old Testament and the New Testament. Muslims had the Koran, which included references to the Old and New Testaments.

Second, all three religions were *monotheistic*. That means that they believed in the existence of only one God. The members of all three religions also believed in salvation, in the possibility of a happy life and future existence prepared by God for those who were faithful.

Relations between these three religions were not always peaceful. At times the Muslims sought to convert Christians and Jews by force. Sometimes they harassed their non-Muslim subjects in other ways. At times Christians oppressed Muslims and tried to force them to convert to Christianity; and over and over again they treated Jews harshly.

ENNA

ME

CONSTANTINOPLE

DAMASCUS

JERUSALEM

CAIRO

MEDINA

MECCA

CHRISTIAN

MUSLIM

HEBREW

In spite of conflict between the followers of these three religions, there were also ongoing business and trading contacts, important exchanges of information and learning, and even conversions from one religion to another. World history would be deeply influenced by the religious and cultural experiences of those peoples who lived through this encounter in the Mediterranean area.

Outline by Chapter
The End of the Ancient World

Chapters		Dates
1	The Roman Empire: beginning of the breakup	400
2	John Chrysostom, bishop of Constantinople	344-407
3-6	The story of Andreas, a young merchant of Constantinople	c. 400
7-9	Ambrose, bishop of Milan and doctor of the Church	340-397
10-12	Augustine, bishop of Hippo and doctor of the Church	354-430
13	The barbarian invasion of the Roman Empire	c. 406 and onward
14	Augustine's opposition to Pelagianism	410 and onward
15	Augustine's great book, *The City of God*	413-426
16	Augustine's death; conquest of Hippo by Vandal tribes	430
17	Jerome, doctor of the Church and translator of the Bible	342-420
18	The Council of Ephesus	431
19	The Council of Chalcedon	451
20-21	Pope Leo the Great	440-461
22	Christianity in Britain	
23	Patrick, Apostle of Ireland	c. 389- c. 461

Chapters		Dates
24	The end of the Roman Empire in the West	476
25	Changes in social, economic, and agricultural life in the Western Empire	410 and onward
26	Persecution of Catholic Christians in Africa under Arian Vandals	429- c. 500
27	Conversion of Clovis, king of the Franks	c. 496
28	Growth of the Church in Frankish lands	
29	Caesar, bishop of Arles	470-542
30-31	Theodoric, Ostrogothic ruler of the West	493-526
32	Gelasius's affirmation of the spiritual authority of the pope	492-496
33	Cassiodorus, preserver of ancient learning	c. 490- c. 580
34-37	Benedict and Scholastica; the origin of the Benedictine Order	c. 480- c. 550/c. 543
38	Revival of the Byzantine Empire under Justinian	527-565
39	Constantinople, center of culture, art, education	
40	The Code of Justinian	529
41	Justinian's reconquest of the West	

Chapters		Dates
42	Architecture under Justinian	
43	Byzantine art under Justinian	
44-45	Religious developments in the Eastern Empire: The Coptic Church The Armenian Church The Nestorian Church of Persia	451 and onward
46	Religious devotion in the Byzantine Church	
47	North Africa reclaimed from the Vandals by Justinian's army	533
48	Continuing conflict between Catholic and Arian Christians under Leovigild, king of the Visigoths	568 and onward
49	Changes in parish life throughout the Church	
50-53	Growth and development of the Church in Gaul	500 and onward
54-55	Arabia at the end of the sixth century	
56-59	Mohammed and the origin of Islam; the rise of the Muslim Empire	c. 610 and onward

Note to Readers: The *c.* before some dates is an abbreviation for *circa*, meaning "about" or "approximately."